Advance Praise

"Love is foundational to wisdom. Love is the force that binds us together and requires an active choice to create a better world. Rumi, the Thirteenth Century philosopher and poet, is fortunate in his latest expositor. Author Chris Parker gently presents and applies the timeless wisdom of Rumi to shape the future of leadership with empathy and authenticity."
- **AMY C. EDMONDSON,** Novartis Professor of Leadership and Management, Harvard Business School, and Author of Right Kind of Wrong: The Science of Failing Well

"Lead from Love with Rumi is an essential guide for anyone looking to reinvent themselves with inspiration from the timeless wisdom of Rumi. This book provides profound insights on leading with compassion and authenticity, helping individuals navigate today's complexities with an authentically heart-centered approach. By reflecting on Rumi's teachings, Parker inspires us to foster meaningful and impactful relationships, transforming our professional lives from the inside out."
- **CHIP CONLEY** New York Times Bestselling Author and Founder of the Modern Elder Academy

"As an entrepreneur and a leader, I've learned more from the 13th-century mystic poet Rumi than from all of the modern business books I've read combined; but now, in this book, author Chris Parker offers a simple yet powerful distillation of Rumi's wisdom for a business context, and the result is a genuinely beautiful book that teaches as much about life and love as business and leadership... although in the end, what's the difference anyway?"
- **BRIAN J ROBERTSON** Founder of Holacracy

"Lead with Love offers bite-size chunks of wisdom! For everyone who is looking for inspiration to approach leadership in a different way."
- **JEROEN DE FLANDER** Bestselling Author of The Art of Performance

"This book invites you to fully embrace who you aspire to be and to inspire others from a place of love, intelligence, and spiritual depth. It provides words to what lies deeply within you, helping you recognize and express your potential to lead from love. By guiding you on a journey to self-realization, the book encourages you to create ripples of positive impact in the world around you. Ultimately, it challenges you to find the courage to live authentically and lead with love, fostering a better world for everyone."
- **KAREN DE BOECK** Lean/Agile Coach and Adjugo Partner

"In 'Lead from Love with Rumi', Chris Parker rediscovers what it is to be human and what that means for our behavior as leaders, followers, and inhabitants of the world. A must-read for anyone caught between the conflicting forces of working life: the need to perform, office politics, and the wish to find a purpose."
- **SIMON BROD** Movement Teacher, Strategy Advisor and Poet

"Chris keeps surprising me with fresh perspectives on leadership and organizational growth. When he told me about his plan to incorporate love into the leadership equation, it felt like a natural progression in his journey as both a person and a leader. This book delves into the importance of doing what you love with the people you care about, and through it, Chris invites you to explore this often underestimated facet of modern leadership."
- **WIM LUBBERSEN** Management Consultant and B&B Owner

"There are countless books on successful and conscious leadership, but 'Lead from Love with Rumi' captures the essence of what leaders and individuals should aspire to in their careers and lives. It is not just another guide to success, but a heartfelt invitation to embark on a new journey – one that starts within. This book seamlessly connects the desire for divine love with the challenges of the business world. Leadership becomes an opportunity to inspire others by embracing a deep love for humanity. 'Lead from Love with Rumi' reminds us that the world needs more leaders who lead for the sake of love, not just for success."
- **DANIELA HOFBAUER** HR Manager and Career Coach

"The most important driver of employee engagement is the extent to which employees believe their leaders have a sincere interest in their wellbeing. Caring and connection is the recipe for success that Chris Parker shares in 'Lead From Love With Rumi.' Packed with simple lessons, this book will transform your approach to leading with heart."
- **STAN PHELPS CSP** Author of the Goldfish Series of Books

"'Lead from Love with Rumi' is a kind invitation to expand our consciousness to reflect love inspired, compassionate leadership; A gentle guide to awaken the essence of our specific life purpose, embody our soul and make it visible in the world so that we can truly lead and live the life that we came to experience and wholeheartedly belong."
- **JYOTISH PATEL** Wholeness Guide, Facilitator of Transformation

"'Lead from Love with Rumi' is not just a leadership manual; it's a guide to personal and professional transformation. It challenges leaders to rethink their approach to power, encouraging a shift from traditional hierarchical models to more inclusive, empathetic and embodied styles of leadership."
- **CHARLOTTE MADER** Executive Coach & Mindfulness Instructor

"'Lead from Love with Rumi' by Chris Parker takes readers on a powerful journey to discover the essence of true leadership through the lens of Rumi's timeless poetry. One of my favorite quotes of Rumi is "If everything around seems dark, look again, you may be the light." Chris masterfully uses this quote to illustrate that in times of struggle or uncertainty, the solutions often lie within us. Instead of seeking external validation or fearing the unknown, this book calls us to turn inward and find our own light – using it to face adversity and act with compassion. Chris blends Rumi's profound wisdom with practical leadership insights, making this a book I would recommend to anyone aiming to lead wholeheartedly."
- **DOROTA KLOP-SOWINSKA** Executive Career Coach and Author of Career Jump! How to Successfully Change your Professional Path

"Anyone who has had the opportunity to meet Chris Parker in person will quickly realize that his invitation to embark on the 'Love Journey' is not a cover for weakness or a shield for his own fears and anxieties. With the physical presence of a U.S. football player and a sharp, witty intellect, Chris's embrace of love is far from a defense mechanism of a fragile personality. His invitation is compelling, made even more so by the fact that his life story clearly shows he practices what he preaches. I am honored to call him a friend, mentor, and business partner!"
- **DIDIER MARLIER** Enablers Network Partner

"Chris Parker successfully translates and elaborates the wisdom and poetry from Rumi in inspiring views and approaches for those who have the privilege to lead others in business or elsewhere. At the core, the book makes clear that leadership comes from the heart, from love. It starts with connecting with your own heart and spirit, with the goodness in yourself as well as your pain - then to the hearts of your fellows in your team, company, etc. True leadership engages, stimulates, inspires, enlightens - this can only be based on love. A baseline that Chris takes further in many aspects of modern business leadership, creating stimulating guidelines for making work and life 'in the Office' to a playful, engaging and positive environment for business-, social- and spiritual growth."
- **GERPHIL KERKHOF** Therapist and Coach

"In 'Lead from Love with Rumi', Chris Parker invites you to have a different look on leadership. In a special way - which love always is - it inspires you to have the courage to be who you are for yourself and also towards others. One of the best things about this book is that you can open it to one of the hundred essays to be inspired and to understand the purpose why you opened that page. As an author myself, I know how uncomfortable and vulnerable you can feel during the whole process. When you read this book, you will also experience how Chris embraced those feelings in an act of self-leadership from love."
- **JESSICA VAN BEEK** Qhuba Sustainability Consultant and Beekeeper

LEAD FROM LOVE WITH RUMI

The word "eshgh" (عشق) is a Persian (Farsi) word that translates to "love" in English. It specifically refers to a deep, passionate, and intense form of love, often with connotations of spiritual or divine love. This word in Persian is included on the cover of the book to show respect to the history and origin of the poetry that inspired the essays.

Rumi primarily wrote his masterpieces in Persian; however, he also wrote in Arabic, Turkish and Greek. In standard Arabic, the same word (عشق) is translated to "eshq" and has a similar depth of meaning, often evoking the notion of an overwhelming, all-encompassing love that transcends mere affection and enters the realm of spiritual and mystical devotion.

LEAD FROM LOVE WITH RUMI

عشق

100 Insights for Leaders to
Harness the Power of Compassion,
Connection and Creativity

CHRIS PARKER

Lead from Love with Rumi
100 Insights for Leaders to Harness the Power of Compassion, Connection and Creativity

ISBN: 979-8-9913434-0-4 Hardcover
ISBN: 979-8-9913434-1-1 Paperback
ISBN: 979-8-9913434-2-8 Ebook

Library of Congress Control Number: 2024918522

Published Ebullient Business Designers in the United States.
Printed by IngramSpark

First edition 2024
10 9 8 7 6 5 4 3 2 1

Cover art by Harshad Kumar at HR Motion Design
Portrait by Jentien ten Heuvel

This book contains excerpts from English translations of the poetry of Jalāl ad-Dīn Muhammad Rūmī. These excerpts are used in accordance with the fair use doctrine for purposes of commentary, criticism, and scholarly discussion. Only portions of the poems are included, rather than complete works, to provide context and enhance the thematic exploration within this book. See the 'About Translations' section for more information.

The essays are inspired by various business and personal development themes, concepts and practices that are outlined in the 'Sources of Concepts and Methods' section.

This book was edited using advanced artificial intelligence tools. While AI technology was employed to enhance the editing process, all interpretations and applications presented in this work are entirely original and solely created by the author.

Special editions of this book are possible with custom covers and forewords by special guests or company executives. For information about special discounts for bulk purchase and customizing versions of the book for company gifts or for information on booking the author for an event, please visit our website at www.ebullient.com/leadfromlove/

For Melanie

While we met at work and fell in love,
this is not the kind of love this book is about...

♥

The profound relationship between Shams of Tabriz and Rumi is one of the most significant spiritual partnerships in history. Shams, a wandering dervish, met Rumi in 1244 and their bond transformed Rumi from a respected scholar into a passionate poet and mystic. Shams' unconventional teachings and deep spiritual insights inspired Rumi to delve into the mysteries of divine love and inner transformation.

This encounter ignited a profound internal journey for Rumi, leading to his creation of some of the world's most cherished mystical poetry. A book inspired by Rumi would be incomplete without highlighting the important influence of this relationship.

East, west, south, or north makes little difference.

No matter what your destination, just be sure to make every

journey, a journey within.

If you travel within, you'll visit the whole full world and

beyond.

- SHAMS of TABRIZ

Contents

Acknowledgements

The earliest memory I have of a manager leading from what I now call love is Tom Carey. Tom shared with me the wisdom to connect people to the work they are most passionate about and then, as a manager, to support them when truly necessary. This simple yet profound approach has stayed with me throughout my career and serves as a foundational principle in this book.

In more recent years, the journey mixed my search for simplicity with deep personal development was triggered through work with Inès Gaston-Echeverria (inesgaston.com). It was through her guidance that I encountered the transformative insights of Abraham Hicks.

A heartfelt thank you goes to Jyotish Patel for his exceptional energy coaching (jyotishpatel.com). His guidance has profoundly influenced my understanding of personal energy and its impact on leadership. Moreover, his sharing the teachings of Dr. Joe Dispenza opened new avenues of thought and practice, enriching the concepts explored in this book.

Additionally, I extend my deepest gratitude to Gerphil Kerkhof for his life coaching (essentialwaves.nl), which provided invaluable guidance and support, helping me navigate the complexities of balancing personal growth with professional aspirations.

Special recognition is due to my collaborator networks of Enablers, Qhuba, and Adjugo, who have been instrumental in bringing this book to life.

From Enablers (enablersnetwork.com), a special thanks to Charlotte Mader, whose steadfast accountability kept me on track during the final stages of this project. Her encouragement and support were invaluable in crossing the finish line. I am deeply grateful to the Qhuba team (qhuba.com) – Jessica van Beek, Simon Brod, Wim Lubbersen, and Wouter Hasekamp. Their collective wisdom and insights have enriched my understanding of the world immeasurably. Similarly, the Adjugo (adjugo.com) team led by Karen De Boeck and

I

Chris Verlinden deserves special mention. Their engaging spirit and dedication to cultivating positive change in their journey have been a beacon of inspiration throughout this process.

I owe a debt of gratitude to Jeroen De Flander (jeroen-de-flander.com), whose sage advice steered the focus of this book. He encouraged me to stretch further into the "why" of leadership, rather than just the mechanics of management. His perspective inspired me to rethink the shape and core message of this work.

Vahid Daemi, the former CEO of LeasePlan (now ayvens.com), has been a pillar of faith and support over the years. His belief in me has been unwavering, and it was his suggestion to study Rumi's teachings on love that provided the profound source of inspiration for this book. Vahid's influence and encouragement have been pivotal in my journey as a leader.

A special thanks to Mohamed Elmasry, Mohammad Hassan, and the Tactful AI team (tactful.ai) in Egypt. Their embodiment of leading from love in their work and interactions has been a powerful example. Their experiences and insights have deeply informed the concepts explored in this book, including the weaving of religious beliefs into leadership as shared by Rumi long ago.

I wish to express my deepest gratitude to Rumi himself, whose timeless wisdom has been a guiding light on this journey of leading from love. I am particularly thankful to Coleman Barks, whose masterful interpretations have made Rumi's teachings accessible to a broader audience.

To all who have been part of this journey, your contributions, whether large or small, have been invaluable. This book is as much a reflection of your influence as it is of my own efforts. Thank you for your continued support and for believing in the vision of leading from love.

Foreword

First and foremost, Chris's interpretation and exploration of Rumi's poetry and its profound message are both extensive and thought-provoking. It is evident that he has endeavored – and succeeded – in moving beyond the superficial, delving deeply into the spiritual aspects of Rumi's teachings.

Furthermore, his application of the principles of love to leadership and business emerges from a genuine desire to incorporate love into his daily professional activities. I believe he has achieved this integration with sincerity and purpose. True humanity encompasses love, and love, in turn, can permeate every aspect of one's life.

During a lunch with Chris in London discussing his book ambitions, we discussed the concept of love and how it might be applied to daily life. I suggested that he might find inspiration in the poetry and writings of the great Persian Sufi poet, Rumi. I have always found Rumi's work to be both inspiring and deeply resonant with the message of spiritual love for humanity.

Later, I was pleased to learn that Chris had indeed incorporated Rumi's poetry into his book about leading from love. Initially, I must admit, I was curious – and somewhat skeptical – about how the concepts of business leadership and spiritual love could be reconciled. Although modern leadership theories emphasize the importance of caring for people and society, I could not envision how love could be woven into this framework.

As Chris himself acknowledges, the discovery of love and its application to leadership is a journey. He has taken significant and inspiring steps toward this goal, and his work serves as a guide for others on this path. I highly recommend this book to all readers who wish to participate in a journey of self-discovery and love.

- VAHID DAEMI

Preface

'Leading from Love with Rumi' is a study into the possibilities of love being a foundation for leadership. It serves as a reflection of my own journey, an exploration of how these powerful forces can intertwine and elevate each other. This is not because I have mastered this approach in life… but because I aspire to this reality. The path of leading from love is one I am still walking, learning, and evolving with each step. I hope that through this exploration, I can share with you the transformative potential I have glimpsed.

I have come to understand that leadership transcends the confines of traditional management science. My career in management and coaching has shown me that true leadership encompasses more than intellectual prowess and strategic acumen. It involves an emotional and spiritual depth that connects us to our teams and our mission in profound ways. The insights in this book are distilled from years of observing, learning, and growing in roles that challenged me to lead with mind, body and soul.

In crafting this book, I have consciously avoided including anecdotes or stories. Such narratives often trigger judgment and opinion, which can distract from the core message. Instead, I have left the application of these principles up to you, the reader. I trust that you will find your own unique ways to integrate these insights into your life and work.

As with any leader, I have benefited from the wisdom and guidance of mentors and teachers along the way. The essays are standing on the shoulders of these giants and my deep desire is this work becomes a symbol of respect and appreciation for these inspirational guides such as Rumi and others listed at in the appendix.

My desire is that this book continues to inspire me when I need a reminder that leading from love is always available. Whether in moments of triumph or challenge, the principles explored here are a source of guidance and strength. They remind me that love is not a passive force but an active, dynamic approach to leadership that can transform our interactions and outcomes.

The first part of the book is a short introduction on how to lead from love and is recommended to understand the context of leadership and love as applied in the essays. The following parts of the book are the 100 essays. While the essays are grouped by topic, my dream when preparing the book is that I will pick it up in the future and open to any of the essays at random and be inspired by what the universe has to offer.

I believe you will find inspiration too. As you read, I encourage you to open your heart and mind to the possibilities that leading from love can bring. Let this book be a companion on your journey, a reminder that the power of love is always within reach, ready to guide you through every decision and interaction. May it inspire you to lead with compassion, courage, and authenticity, and to create a ripple effect of positive change in your organization and beyond.

From love,
- CHRIS PARKER

You are invited to share your reflections and feedback! Please visit the following website: www.ebullient.com/leadfromlove/.

The Business Simplicity Podcast includes episodes with Chris Parker having conversations with leaders from around the world about their favorite Rumi quote and how it inspires them.

Connect on LinkedIn: https://www.linkedin.com/in/simplychrisparker/

LEAD FROM LOVE WITH RUMI

Introducing Leading From Love

At its essence, love transcends the surface and reaches into the depths of the human spirit, removing barriers that disconnect us from our inner source of truth and beauty. It binds us to our most authentic selves, lighting our path with clarity and compassion.

In leadership, love becomes a guiding force, much like a lighthouse offering hope and anticipation. While fear or coercion may yield temporary results, they come at a significant cost. In contrast, love fosters genuine connection and unwavering support, leading to true greatness. Leaders who lead with love cultivate environments where trust and respect thrive, enabling teams to surpass their limits and achieve extraordinary outcomes.

Love is an endless source of energy, fueling authentic connections and nurturing a space where creativity and innovation flourish. This clarity allows for decisions that are both intelligent and compassionate.

Leadership, at its core, is about providing support and direction. It is the art of inspiring and guiding others to reach their highest potential. Great leaders know that true leadership is not about wielding power but about empowering others to discover their own strengths. When grounded in love, this leadership style creates a ripple effect, spreading positivity and fostering a culture of growth and collaboration.

Leadership emerges from self-love

Leading from love begins with leading yourself. Self-love is the foundation of authentic leadership. A leader cannot truly lead others from love without first loving themselves – this means accepting both strengths and flaws, understanding personal needs and desires, and finding peace with one's journey. When a leader loves themselves, they exude a calm confidence that others naturally trust and follow.

Effective leadership also respects the unique journey of each team member. Leaders who lead from love recognize the individual talents and aspirations of their team, offering encouragement and support that empowers others to reach their full potential – leaving a lasting impact that shapes both careers and lives. True leaders engage with the person beneath the behavior, recognizing the inherent worth and potential within each individual. They address challenges with compassion and wisdom, crafting solutions that honor the humanity of everyone involved.

What you pay attention to grows

What you choose to focus on significantly shapes the outcomes you experience. It's often said that we find what we expect. If you've already decided that a task will be hard, you'll likely encounter more obstacles and problems. However, if you decide it will be easy, solutions begin to reveal themselves through the power of synchronicity. This isn't magic – it's the product of mindset and awareness. The reality you create as a leader is deeply tied to the expectations you set.

Mindset serves as the foundation for everything. A leader's thoughts and beliefs shape not only their personal reality but also the environment for those they lead. When you focus on potential, solutions, and success, you nurture an atmosphere where possibilities emerge effortlessly. On the contrary, when you dwell on difficulty or failure, you create a self-fulfilling prophecy, where challenges grow and dominate your experience. Your energy follows your attention, and where that attention goes, growth follows – be it in the form of opportunity or obstacle.

There's a delicate paradox a leader must navigate: the expectation of fostering greatness in others while not seeking validation or love in return. This balance requires a deep understanding of human nature and a commitment to unconditional support and growth. It's about holding the space for each individual to grow into their best version while not depending on their approval or admiration. When you are aligned with your own true self, clarity in decision-making follows naturally. In this space of self-security, you lead from a place of integrity, creating an environment where others can also find themselves.

Security, wholeness, and wellness in leadership come from being in sync with your own being. When you are aligned internally, your external actions reflect this balance, creating harmony within your team. As a leader, your role is to stay connected to this inner truth, holding the intention for others to grow while trusting that their journey will unfold in its own time. Leading from this place of clarity encourages the team to thrive and perform at their highest potential.

Tension is necessary and welcome

Tensions and conflicts arise in business, just like in any relationship, and this contrast gives us insights into what to invest further into and what needs to change. These moments of friction are not to be feared but embraced as opportunities for growth and deeper understanding. A leader who leads from love approaches conflict with an open mind and a compassionate heart, seeking to understand the root causes and find solutions that honor the needs and aspirations of all involved.

Avoiding conflict is not leading from love; it is, in fact, a form of avoidance that stifles growth. Leading with love means having the courage to confront uncomfortable situations with clarity and grace, knowing that true leadership involves fostering an environment where discomfort is transformed into dialogue, and tension becomes a gateway to discovery. Without conflict, we miss the opportunity to learn, both about ourselves and others. Through friction, we gain a deeper understanding of different perspectives, sharpen our problem-solving skills, and evolve as individuals and as a team.

One of the primary functions of a business organization is to offer individuals the gift of conflict as a source of inspiration and growth. Conflict forces us to re-examine our assumptions, refine our ideas, and innovate solutions that wouldn't have surfaced in a perfectly harmonious environment. When seen through this lens, conflict is not something to dread but a critical part of the creative process. It fuels development, innovation, and the evolution of both the individual and the collective.

Leaders who understand this invite tension and conflict into the conversation, not as disruptions, but as necessary ingredients for progress. By creating a safe space where team members can express dissenting views, raise concerns, or question decisions, leaders foster a culture of openness, trust, and respect. In this environment, teams are encouraged to lean into discomfort, knowing that growth often lies just beyond the edge of what is familiar or comfortable.

Conflict, approached with love and empathy, can also deepen relationships. It provides an opportunity to truly see and understand one another. When we resolve conflict through dialogue that honors each individual's perspective, we strengthen the bonds of trust within the team. It creates a foundation where individuals feel valued for their unique contributions and are motivated to bring their full selves to the table.

The key is not to shy away from tension but to embrace it as a powerful teacher. When a leader frames conflict as an opportunity for collective growth rather than a personal attack, the entire team benefits. Individuals learn to approach challenges with an open heart and mind, knowing that they are part of a shared journey toward continuous improvement and mutual understanding.

Your emotions guide the way

The emotions of a leader serve as one of the most powerful tools for navigating the complexities of leadership. They act as a guidance system, signaling whether or not you are aligned with the principles of leading from love. When a leader experiences stress, discomfort, or unease, it often indicates a misalignment with their core values and the compassionate foundation of leadership. These negative emotions are a red flag, showing that the leader may be reacting from fear, control, or ego rather than from a place of love. Recognizing these emotional signals early can help a leader recalibrate and return to a place of authenticity and compassion.

In contrast, a leader who feels calm, satisfied, and at peace, even in the midst of difficult decisions, is operating in alignment with their true values. This state of emotional balance reflects a connection to one's inner self – a place where decisions are made with both intelligence and compassion. When a leader trusts their emotions and allows them to guide their choices, they foster an environment where clarity and wisdom prevail. This emotional equilibrium allows them to address challenges with grace and resilience, seeing obstacles not as threats, but as opportunities for growth.

Operating from self-love further strengthens a leader's emotional guidance system. When grounded in self-love, a leader can trust their intuition and inner voice to make decisions that resonate with compassion and integrity. In this state, intuition becomes a trusted ally, helping the leader navigate uncertainty and complexity with confidence. This connection to their emotions not only benefits the leader personally but also creates a ripple effect, encouraging their team to trust their own emotions and approach their work with authenticity and empathy.

Rational, emotional and spiritual power

When all dimensions of a leader – rational, emotional, and spiritual – are fully present, they can harmoniously contribute to that leader's truth. This integration empowers a leader to approach challenges with authenticity and confidence, even in the face of difficult topics or tough decisions. Leading from love does not mean avoiding hardship or being overly soft. In fact, it often requires the opposite: a leader must be brutally tough when necessary. Holding yourself and others accountable is an essential aspect of leadership, and believing in a person's capacity to achieve more than they realize is an act of love. This balance of firmness and compassion allows a leader to set high expectations while providing the support needed to meet them.

A leader's rational mind plays a crucial role in setting clear goals, developing strategic plans, and measuring progress. Leading from love does not exclude rationality, strategy, or productivity; it embraces them. These elements are enhanced by love because a leader who operates from this place uses rational thinking not to exert control, but to celebrate achievements and identify areas for growth. Professionalism, in this context, is not a rigid standard but a reflection of respect and integrity in every interaction. Love amplifies the effectiveness of these logical tools, guiding a leader to make decisions that are grounded in reason while remaining aligned with empathy and care.

The emotional dimension of leadership adds another layer of depth to decision-making. Leaders who embrace emotional intelligence can engage deeply with their teams, understanding the motivations, fears, and aspirations of each member. This emotional connection allows leaders to hold tough conversations with authenticity, knowing that addressing hard topics from a place of love fosters growth and resilience. It's about setting boundaries, offering constructive feedback, and encouraging personal accountability, all while maintaining a compassionate and empathetic stance. A leader who taps into their emotional power can navigate the nuances of human behavior, making tough decisions without sacrificing trust or mutual respect.

Spiritual power, the often-overlooked dimension of leadership, brings clarity of purpose and alignment with one's inner truth. When a leader is spiritually grounded, they are better equipped to trust the process, even when outcomes are uncertain. This deep connection to their higher self provides clarity in the face of ambiguity and encourages a sense of peace amidst difficult decisions. Leaders who engage from this space not only inspire others but also create environments where authenticity, innovation, and trust thrive.

What is now is perfect

To lead effectively, embrace who you are in this moment – not who you were in the past or who you aspire to be in the future. This means acknowledging your journey, understanding that growth is an ongoing process, and accepting yourself fully as you are today. It is through this self-awareness that your actions and decisions are guided with authenticity and clarity.

Leading from love involves offering support and guidance from a place of calm confidence. This inner state allows a leader to cultivate remarkable creativity while making tough decisions with compassion. When you lead from this place, you create an environment where others feel safe to be their authentic selves, enabling boldness and innovation to flourish. This sense of calm confidence transforms the workplace into a space of trust and creativity, where the seemingly impossible becomes attainable, and individuals are inspired to reach their highest potential.

The daily path of leading from love is about staying deeply grounded, calm, and connected to your inner being, while maintaining a clear intention for something greater to emerge from the unknown. This leader does not act out of fear or past regrets but from a sense of satisfaction and acceptance of the present. It is this calm, compassionate presence that defines a leader who leads from love. They approach each challenge and opportunity with fulfillment, knowing that every moment offers a chance to learn, grow, and evolve.

Outcomes are always mysterious

Leading from love means recognizing that outcomes are often difficult, if not impossible, to predict. Leadership isn't about having all the answers upfront but about staying adaptable and open to the journey as it unfolds. Flexibility becomes crucial. This doesn't mean abandoning strategies or plans altogether, but rather holding them lightly – ready to pivot when new information, challenges, or opportunities arise. Leaders who embody this mindset create a culture where change is embraced, not feared. Their teams become more resilient, always prepared to face the unexpected with confidence and creativity.

While strategies and plans provide essential direction and a baseline to measure progress, reality tends to unfold differently than anticipated. Conflicts will emerge along the way, as will unexpected challenges. These are not to be viewed as failures but as integral parts of the journey. A leader's mindset – grounded in love, flexibility, and openness – will determine how they navigate these obstacles. The ability to adjust and adapt the plan in response to real-time experiences is what allows a team to succeed despite the unpredictability.

Love, at its core, is open to the unknown and mysterious. It embraces the fact that not everything can be. This openness gives leaders the ability to see possibilities where others might see only problems. It fosters the creativity to find solutions in unlikely places and to remain calm and centered in the midst of chaos. The ability to embrace uncertainty doesn't mean disregarding strategy – it means trusting that even when the path is unclear, there is inherent potential in every moment.

Leaders who trust the process, even when the outcome is unknown, inspire the same level of confidence in their teams. Embracing the mystery means understanding that leadership is not a straight line but a dynamic, evolving process. It's about being present, adapting quickly, and believing in the possibilities that lie beyond immediate challenges. This faith in the journey, combined with a flexible strategy, allows teams to thrive amidst uncertainty and continually move forward with purpose.

You are the change

If your workplace isn't vibrating with love, remember that the change can only start with you. Leadership emerges from self-love, and by embracing this foundation, you can lead from a place of authenticity, clarity, and compassion. Leading from love means allowing these principles to shape your actions, your interactions, and your overall attitude. Even small shifts in your behavior – such as showing empathy, practicing appreciation, and prioritizing genuine connections – can create ripples that gradually influence your entire organization.

Leadership is not about waiting for others to act. Just as self-love creates the internal strength to lead authentically, taking the initiative to lead from love can inspire others to follow. By setting an example through your own commitment to compassion, empathy, and integrity, you demonstrate what's possible. You hold the power to transform not only yourself but the culture and dynamics of your team. The ripple effect of your actions can foster a thriving, connected, and positive workplace environment.

Be the change. Just as self-love lays the groundwork for personal leadership, embodying the qualities of love and compassion in your professional life allows you to lead others with the same strength. There is no external force that can make this shift – it is an internal choice. By leading from love, you create an environment where others feel empowered to do the same, gradually cultivating a culture that thrives on respect, collaboration, and trust. Through your dedication, the entire organization can transform into a community where love, creativity, and connection flourish.

Inspired by Rumi

Rumi's teachings are perfectly aligned with the philosophy of leading from love, as both emphasize the transformative power of the heart and the importance of reconnecting with our true selves. Rumi spoke often about the need to peel away the superficial layers that separate us from our inner wisdom. In his view, life should be guided by the heart's clarity and compassion, free from the distractions of ego, fear, and external expectations. This is precisely what leading from love advocates – a leadership style that nurtures self-awareness, empathy, and authenticity.

Rumi's poetry beautifully illustrates the profound change that takes place when we allow love to be the driving force in our lives. His words encourage us to transcend the limitations imposed by fear and ego, leading instead from a place of openness and connection. In the same way, Leading from Love invites leaders to cultivate a deep alignment with their inner truth, enabling them to act from a foundation of love and integrity in their leadership roles.

Both Rumi's teachings and the principles of Leading from Love recognize that love is an inexhaustible source of energy – one that fuels connection, sparks creativity, and provides a deep sense of purpose. This love empowers us to navigate the complexities of leadership and life with grace, wisdom, and a clear sense of direction. As Rumi teaches us to lead our personal lives with compassion and inner clarity, Leading from Love applies these same principles to leadership, creating environments where individuals and organizations can thrive with authenticity and heart.

Leading from love

By embracing love as a guiding principle, we open ourselves to a leadership style that is dynamic, resilient, and deeply human. We learn to adapt quickly, find joy in the present, and anticipate the future with excitement. This journey is about more than improving our leadership skills. It is about evolving into leaders who inspire and uplift, creating environments where everyone can thrive. Let these essays be your companion on this journey, guiding you toward a leadership style that is both powerful and profoundly compassionate.

Where to begin the journey of leading from love? Discover the depths of yourself and the calm and clarity of self-love through meditation before you begin each day. Everyone's meditative practice is different and unique. Find your own moment in the day where you are able to connect with your deeper truth. From that space of compassion, the most powerful practice a leader can do daily when confronted with feelings of fear, uncertainty and tension is to ask themselves the simple question that has been repeated by masters, mentors and leaders throughout the ages...

what would love do?

Insights for Leading Yourself & Your Career

The cure for the pain is in the pain.

This profound statement, while simple in its construct, unravels a deep truth about the human experience, particularly in the intersection of personal development and leadership. When we encounter pain or tension, our first instinct may be to shy away from it, to find the quickest route to safety and comfort. However, real growth, and indeed, the resolution of this tension, demands that we lean into the discomfort, to truly understand and embrace it. Only through this courageous act can we uncover the roots of our issues and begin the healing process.

Leading from love means recognizing that every challenge we face is not a detour on our journey but a part of the path itself. It requires us to acknowledge our vulnerabilities and to see them not as weaknesses but as opportunities for fortification. When we lead with love, we foster an environment where openness is not just encouraged but celebrated. It's an approach that combines the heart's passion with the mind's discernment, creating a powerful synergy that propels us and those around us forward.

In navigating the terrains of our inner landscapes, we must cultivate a balance. This equilibrium isn't found in a static state but in the constant motion of self-reflection, learning, and application. It's the dance between understanding our emotions and harnessing them, between seeking knowledge and embodying wisdom, between aspiring for spiritual growth and grounding it in practical actions. This dynamic balance is what shapes not only effective leaders but transformative ones.

The journey through pain is not one we must walk alone. It invites us to build bridges of empathy, to connect with others on a fundamental level. It calls for a leadership style that is both responsive and responsible, one that views governance not as a hierarchy of power but as a network of empowerment. When we view our roles through this lens, we foster an environment where trust and safety are the norms, where each individual's voice contributes to the harmony of the whole.

As we travel this path, we draw from a wellspring of positive energy. We come to understand that our intentions and beliefs shape our reality. It is not merely the act of attracting what we desire but the deeper practice of becoming what we aspire to be. We become architects of our destiny, crafting it with the bricks of our thoughts, the mortar of our emotions, and the blueprint of our spiritual insights.

Embracing our pain is not the end of our journey but a passage to a new beginning, where every lesson is a stepping stone to a higher version of ourselves. It is here, in the heart of our challenges, that we find the keys to unlocking our fullest potential, leading from a place of love, and inspiring those around us to do the same.

If light is in your heart,
you will find your way home.

In the vast expanse of the business world, where paths often diverge and destinations remain obscured by the fog of uncertainty, there lies an eternal truth. This truth whispers softly, reminding us that the key to navigating this labyrinth lies not in the external markers of success but within ourselves. It suggests that the more connected we are to our inner essence, the clearer our journey becomes, guiding us toward not just any working environment, but one that resonates deeply with our core values and aspirations.

Leading from love, we begin to understand that this connection to our inner self acts as the compass that points us towards our true north. It's a journey that starts with self-awareness, a profound understanding of our strengths, weaknesses, and, most importantly, our values. This awareness does not come overnight but is a result of continuous introspection, a willingness to confront our fears, and the courage to embrace our vulnerabilities. It is in this process of self-discovery that we begin to illuminate the light within us, making our path clearer and our decisions more aligned with our true selves.

This inner light serves as a beacon, attracting opportunities and environments that are in harmony with our essence. It enables us to discern not only the kind of work that fulfills us but also the kind of people and cultures that uplift us. When we operate from a place of authenticity, we naturally gravitate towards environments that respect and nurture our individuality, creativity, and well-being. This alignment is the cornerstone of not just professional success but personal fulfillment and happiness.

This profound connection to ourselves enhances our ability to lead with empathy. It fosters a leadership style that is not authoritarian but collaborative, one that values diversity of thought and encourages innovation. It's a leadership that understands the power of human-centered design, recognizing that the most successful organizations are those that put their people first, creating a culture where everyone feels seen, heard, and valued.

The journey to finding a wonderful working environment starts with lighting the path from within. It's a journey that requires us to peel away the layers of societal expectations and professional pressures to uncover our true desires and aspirations. By leading with love and authenticity, we not only find our way home to a place that mirrors our inner landscape but also inspire those around us to embark on their journey of self-discovery. In doing so, we create not just a better working environment but a better world, one heart at a time.

You are searching the world for treasure,

but the real treasure is yourself.

In a world bustling with the chase for material wealth, it's easy to forget the most valuable asset we possess: ourselves. We descend into the depths of the earth, scale the highest mountains, and traverse the widest seas in search of treasures, oblivious to the fact that the greatest treasure lies within. This realization beckons a transformative journey, not just in the way we work, but in the essence of how we perceive value, success, and fulfillment. It's a call to awaken to our inherent potential, to recognize that what we exchange for a wage is but a fraction of our true capacity.

Leading from love, the journey inward reveals a landscape rich with untapped talent, creativity, and passion. It's a discovery that shifts the paradigm from seeking external validation to nurturing our internal wealth. This awakening is not a solitary endeavor. It is a collective voyage that encourages us to look beyond the superficial metrics of success and to foster an environment where everyone is empowered to explore and express their fullest potential. It's about crafting spaces where vulnerability is not a weakness but a cornerstone for innovation, where trust prevails over fear, and where every individual is seen as a whole person, not just a role or a function.

Embracing this perspective transforms the workplace from a transactional space into a transformative one. It's where the conventional exchange of time for money is enriched with opportunities for personal growth, purposeful engagement, and genuine connections. This transformation is not just beneficial for the individuals; it becomes the bedrock of organizational resilience, adaptability, and creativity. It's the kind of environment that attracts and retains talent not just through competitive wages, but through the promise of being part of something larger than yourself, of contributing to a shared vision that celebrates each person's unique contribution.

This shift requires courage. It demands that we shed the layers of societal conditioning that equate success with accumulation and recognize that our worth is not determined by our productivity or possessions. It's a redefinition of wealth that includes emotional well-being, intellectual growth, and spiritual fulfillment. It's an acknowledgment that when we align our work with our inner treasure, we don't just achieve success; we redefine it.

The quest for external treasures is a reflection of our yearning for deeper, more meaningful connections with ourselves and the world around us. It's a journey back to our essence, to the understanding that the real treasure has been with us all along. By embracing this truth, we unlock the full spectrum of our potential, turning every endeavor into an opportunity for growth, every challenge into a lesson, and every interaction into a chance to make a meaningful difference.

Your task is not to seek for love,

but merely to seek and find all

the barriers within yourself that

you have built against it.

In the game of career development, we often find ourselves chasing after milestones and accolades, believing that our professional progression is solely a function of our external achievements. This pursuit, driven by societal norms and expectations, can lead us down a path where success is measured by titles, income, and recognition. However, this outward focus overlooks a crucial aspect of true career fulfillment and growth: the journey inward. The real transformation begins not with acquiring more skills or expanding our network but with dismantling the internal barriers that limit our capacity to connect, innovate, and lead.

Leading from love, the essence of our professional journey shifts from achieving to becoming. It invites us to explore the depths of our being, to uncover and dismantle the walls we have built against our own potential. This process is not about weakening our resolve but about opening ourselves to the richness of our own humanity. It's about recognizing that our greatest asset is not our expertise or accomplishments but our ability to grow, adapt, and connect with others on a meaningful level.

This journey of inward discovery requires a delicate balance between intellectual rigor and compassion, between ambition and humility, between action and reflection. It's a path that celebrates our vulnerabilities as much as our strengths, understanding that leadership is not about perfection but authenticity. By fostering environments where curiosity, compassion, and courage flourish, we not only accelerate our own growth but also inspire those around us to embark on their own journeys of self-discovery.

This approach resonates with the idea that what we attract in our careers is a reflection of our inner state. By aligning our intentions and actions with our deepest values, we create a magnetic force that draws opportunities, relationships, and experiences that are in harmony with our true self. This alignment is not about manipulating outcomes but about embodying the qualities we wish to see in our professional lives.

The path to profound career growth is not linear nor outwardly directed. It's a journey that spirals inward, inviting us to confront and transcend the limitations we have imposed on ourselves. It's about understanding that our capacity for impact and fulfillment is not determined by the accolades we accumulate but by the depth of our inner growth. By embracing this journey, we unlock a wellspring of creativity, resilience, and connection that propels us forward, not just as professionals but as human beings. In doing so, we realize that the most significant barriers to our success are not external challenges but the ones we have built within ourselves.

If everything around seems dark,
look again, you may be the light.

In the shadows of a toxic work environment, where negativity seems to cloud every interaction and decision, it can be challenging to see a way forward. The instinct might be to search for external solutions, to wish for a hero to emerge and dispel the darkness. However, the real answer to transforming such an environment often lies not in external changes but within us. It's in the realization that we each possess the potential to be a beacon of positivity, a catalyst for change that can illuminate the path toward a healthier, more supportive workplace.

Leading from love, the journey to dissipate toxicity and nurture a positive work culture starts with self-reflection and a commitment to embody the values we wish to see around us. This approach is not about ignoring the challenges or pretending they don't exist. It is about choosing to respond to them with understanding, empathy, and resilience. By fostering an attitude of compassion and support, we encourage others to open up, share their experiences, and work together towards solutions that benefit everyone.

Creating such a shift requires patience and persistence. It involves actively listening to the concerns of our colleagues, recognizing the validity of their emotions, and working collaboratively to address the underlying issues. It's about setting an example through our actions, demonstrating how to communicate respectfully, offer constructive feedback, and celebrate the achievements of others. By doing so, we slowly but surely cultivate an environment where trust flourishes and where every team member feels valued and heard.

This transformation extends beyond mere interpersonal dynamics. It's about reimagining the very structure of our work environment to promote transparency, accountability, and inclusivity. This might involve advocating for practices that encourage open dialogue, developing policies that support work-life balance, or implementing systems that ensure everyone has a voice in decision-making processes. Through these efforts, we not only address the symptoms of toxicity but also tackle its root causes, laying the foundation for a culture that is both high-performing and humane.

The power to transform a toxic work environment lies within each of us. By choosing to be the light in the darkness, we not only elevate ourselves but also inspire those around us to join in creating a workplace that reflects the best of what we can be. This journey is not without its challenges, but it's through facing these challenges with courage, compassion, and conviction that we discover our true potential to effect meaningful change. In doing so, we prove that the most effective solution to toxicity is not to seek salvation from outside but to nurture it from within, one action, one interaction, at a time.

You have to walk through the darkness
in order to find the light.

Embarking on a career journey often feels like navigating through an uncharted territory, marked by periods of uncertainty and discomfort. It's not uncommon to find yourself in professional environments that feel less than ideal, places that challenge our patience, resilience, and even our sense of purpose. Yet, it's precisely these experiences, the ones we'd rather avoid or escape from, that hold invaluable lessons about who we are and what truly fulfills us. These challenging moments are not merely obstacles; they are crucial chapters in our personal and professional growth narrative, offering clarity and insight that can only be gained through experience.

Leading from love, embracing these less-than-ideal work situations becomes an exercise in self-discovery and personal growth. It's an opportunity to discover the depths of our own resilience, to test our capabilities, and to refine our understanding of what we truly value in our work and life. This approach does not romanticize the struggle but acknowledges it as a necessary part of the journey toward finding our place in the world. It's about learning to navigate through the darkness with grace, understanding that each step, no matter how challenging, is guiding us closer to our light.

The insights gained from these experiences are manifold. They teach us about the kind of work environment in which we thrive, the leadership styles that inspire us, and the company cultures that resonate with our core values. They sharpen our ability to discern between what merely looks appealing on the surface and what genuinely aligns with our aspirations and well-being. This journey, fraught with trials, lays the groundwork for a career built not just on achievements, but on a deep sense of purpose and satisfaction.

This path of discovery fosters a profound appreciation for the contrast in experiences. It illuminates the fact that understanding and appreciating what we truly desire often requires us to first encounter its opposite. It's a process that imbues us with empathy, resilience, and a nuanced perspective on success and fulfillment. By walking through the darkness, we not only find our light but learn to shine it more brightly, guiding not only our own way but also illuminating paths for others.

The journey through less-than-ideal work environments is not a detour or a setback but an integral part of carving out a career that is deeply rewarding and aligned with our true self. It's a journey that teaches us that the light we seek is not found at the destination but kindled within us, step by challenging step. Through this process, we not only discover what we are capable of but also what it means to live and work with authenticity, purpose, and joy.

Beauty surrounds us.

In the whirlwind of deadlines, meetings, and seemingly endless to-do lists, it's easy to lose sight of the beauty that unfolds in the workplace every day. The pressures and challenges can overshadow the moments of triumph, collaboration, and genuine human connection that occur amidst the chaos. Yet, if we pause, even for a moment, to lift our gaze from the immediate tasks at hand, we begin to witness the extraordinary in the ordinary, the beauty that Rumi reminds us of surrounds us always.

Leading from love, the transformation in perspective begins. This shift allows us to see beyond the surface tensions and recognize the intricate dance of relationships, ideas, and successes that define our daily work life. It's in the shared laughter over a cup of coffee, the spark of innovation that lights up a colleague's eyes, and the quiet dedication that hums through the office as deadlines approach. These are the moments where beauty resides, not just in the achievements themselves but in the journey towards them, marked by resilience, teamwork, and a shared sense of purpose.

Acknowledging this beauty does not negate the existence of stress or difficulty but offers a counterbalance that enriches our work experience. It invites us to celebrate the small victories, to appreciate the diversity of thoughts and backgrounds that enrich our projects, and to cultivate an environment where empathy and support are as fundamental as productivity and performance. By fostering this awareness, we not only enhance our own well-being but also contribute to a culture that values and uplifts every member of the team.

This perspective nurtures a sense of gratitude and positivity that can transform challenges into opportunities for growth and learning. It encourages us to approach problems with creativity, to see potential where others might see obstacles, and to draw strength from the community we build within our workplaces. This approach doesn't just make the office a more pleasant place to be; it drives innovation, motivates teams, and ultimately contributes to the success of the organization.

The beauty that surrounds us at work is a testament to the human capacity for resilience, collaboration, and joy. It's a reminder that, even in the midst of stress and uncertainty, we have the power to create moments of significance and connection. By choosing to focus on these moments, to cultivate them and cherish them, we not only make our work lives richer but also bring out the best in ourselves and those around us. It's in this recognition that we find not just beauty, but also the key to a fulfilling and rewarding work experience.

Do not sell your soul in exchange of anything,

this is the only thing you have brought into this world

and the only thing you can take back.

In the curious dynamics of business and personal life, the pursuit of success often brings us to crossroads, where the choices we make can profoundly affect our integrity and ethical stance. Amidst the whirlwind of ambition, competition, and the relentless push for growth, there emerges a timeless counsel: the essence of who we are, our very soul, is not a commodity for trade. This profound realization beckons us to navigate through business and life with unwavering ethics, holding tight to the conviction that our core values are not up for negotiation.

Leading from love, we anchor ourselves in the principles that elevate our actions beyond the mere calculus of profit and loss. It is a leadership ethos that cherishes transparency, honesty, and respect, not just as professional policies but as personal commitments. This approach does not view ethical considerations as constraints but as the very foundation upon which lasting success is built. It recognizes that the trust we inspire in our customers, our teams, and our partners is not just a function of what we achieve but of how we achieve it.

Maintaining the highest level of ethics in business and life is a testament to the balance between logos, ethos, and pathos – between rational decision-making, moral principles, and the inner emotional compass that guides our interactions. It's an acknowledgment that our legacy is defined not by the wealth we accumulate but by the impact of our choices on the world around us and the integrity with which we conduct our lives.

This commitment to ethics resonates deeply with the principles of leading from love, creating environments where people feel valued, respected, and free to express their authentic selves. It fosters a culture where leadership is not about exerting power but about empowering others, where success is measured not just in metrics but in the positive contributions we make to society.

The journey through business and life, guided by the highest ethical standards, is a reflection of our deepest values and the legacy we wish to leave. It is a path that challenges us to rise above the fray, to lead with compassion, and to make choices that honor our soul – the most precious possession we have. This journey, illuminated by the principles of love, simplicity, and integrity, not only enriches our lives but also shapes the world in ways that reflect our most cherished beliefs. It is a reminder that in the pursuit of success, our greatest asset and gift is the unwavering commitment to walk in the light of our truth and values.

By love bitter things become sweet.

In the complex and often challenging world of business, tensions and conflicts are not just inevitable; they are part of the landscape within which we strive for growth, innovation, and success. Yet, it is not the presence of these difficulties that defines our journey but our response to them. When approached from a place of love rather than fear, even the most bitter experiences can transform into opportunities for growth, learning, and deeper connection.

Leading from love, we begin to view the tensions and conflicts that arise not as threats but as invitations to explore new perspectives, to understand deeper undercurrents, and to strengthen relationships through empathy and dialogue. This shift in approach does not mean avoiding difficult conversations or sugarcoating the reality of the challenges faced but engaging with them openly and with a heart guided by compassion and understanding.

This perspective encourages a leadership style that is rooted in leading from love, where the focus is on building bridges rather than walls, on fostering an environment of connectedness where everyone feels valued and heard. It's about recognizing that the true measure of our success lies not just in the outcomes we achieve but in the manner in which we navigate the journey, including how we deal with adversity.

Embracing love as a guiding principle in addressing tensions allows us to tap into a deeper well of creativity and resilience. It encourages us to see beyond the immediate conflict to the potential for transformation and growth, to find sweetness in what initially appeared bitter. This approach aligns with principles of holistic systems thinking, where challenges are viewed as part of an interconnected web of relationships and dynamics, each offering lessons and pathways to improvement.

The journey through business and life, punctuated by moments of tension and conflict, offers a profound opportunity to practice leading from love. It's a reminder that our capacity to transform challenges into opportunities for growth, to find sweetness in the bitter, is amplified by our willingness to approach each situation with an open heart and a spirit of empathy. It is through this lens of love that we can truly appreciate the value of every experience, growing through it and emerging stronger, wiser, and more connected to those around us.

Half of life is lost in charming others.

The other half is lost in going through

anxieties caused by others.

Leave this game.

You have played enough.

In the ever-evolving landscape of business and personal growth, a profound realization beckons – the pursuit of approval and the relentless navigation through anxieties tied to others' expectations often lead us astray from our true path. This realization, deeply embedded in wisdom, invites us to shed the incessant game of seeking external validation and to embrace a journey of self-assuredness and authenticity.

Leading from love, we embark on a transformative path that encourages us to cast aside the shackles of worry about winning or losing specific customers or deals. It is a recognition that the essence of true success lies not in the fleeting victories or defeats but in the confidence with which we walk our path. This confidence, radiating from a place of inner strength and clarity, becomes a beacon, attracting new opportunities and fostering connections that resonate with our core values and vision.

This approach champions the principles of simplicity, urging us to cut through the complexity that often clouds our judgment and actions. By focusing on what truly matters – our mission, our passion, and our integrity – we unlock a powerful alignment between our actions and our deepest intentions. It is here, in this space of alignment, that we find the freedom to innovate, to lead with empathy, and to create a legacy that transcends the transactional nature of business.

Embracing this mindset nurtures a culture of collaboration within our teams and organizations, where individuals feel empowered to express their ideas, to take risks, and to contribute to a collective vision without the fear of judgment. It encourages an environment where harmony thrives, where connections are built on genuine understanding and respect, and where the journey of growth is shared and celebrated.

The invitation to leave behind the game of charming and worrying about the approval of others is an invitation to step into a space of boundless potential. It is a call to walk in confidence, to lead with love, and to open ourselves to the infinite possibilities that arise when we align with our authentic selves. By doing so, we not only elevate our personal and professional lives but also inspire those around us to embark on their own journeys of self-discovery and fulfillment. It is a testament to the power of confidence, simplicity, and love as catalysts for change, growth, and true success.

Find the sweetness in your own heart,

then you may find the sweetness in every heart.

In the voyage of personal and professional development, the journey toward fostering an environment of love and peace begins not outside, but within the caverns of our own hearts. It is in the exploration and nurturing of our inner world that we unlock the capacity to see and inspire the potential for harmony and affection in others. This inward journey, challenging yet rewarding, requires us to cultivate a sanctuary of serenity and love within ourselves, recognizing that true change in the world around us starts with transformation within.

Leading from love, we embark on a path of self-discovery and introspection, where the quest for peace becomes a reflection of our own state of being. It is a journey that demands honesty, vulnerability, and the courage to confront and embrace our own imperfections and fears. In doing so, we cultivate a deep sense of self-love and acceptance, creating a foundation upon which empathy for others can flourish. This process not only enriches our personal lives but also transforms the way we engage with the world, allowing us to approach leadership and relationships with a heart that is open, understanding, and compassionate.

The pursuit of internal harmony guides us in developing our emotional guidance system, an invaluable tool in navigating the complexities of human interactions. It enables us to listen deeply, communicate empathetically, and lead with a sense of purpose that resonates with authenticity and kindness. In fostering an environment of trust, we encourage those around us to share their own journeys, to explore their vulnerabilities without fear of judgment, and to engage in the collective endeavor of building a culture rooted in mutual respect and understanding.

This internal alignment with love and peace acts as a beacon, attracting like-minded individuals and creating communities where the principles of collaboration, and holistic well-being are celebrated and lived. It's a reminder that the energy we emit is often reflected back to us, and by embodying the values of love and peace, we invite those energies into our professional and personal spaces.

The discovery of love and peace within ourselves is not a solitary benefit but a gift that keeps on giving, enriching our interactions, and inspiring those we lead and collaborate with to embark on their own journeys of self-reflection and growth. It is a testament to the idea that to find the sweetness in every heart, we must first uncover and nurture it in our own, leading by example and spreading ripples of positivity and transformation that can transcend boundaries and ignite change.

with love, you don't bargain.

There, the choice is not yours.

Love is a mirror, it reflects only your essence,

if you have the courage to look in its face.

In the landscape of leadership and personal growth, facing the specters of fear and toxicity requires more than just strategic acumen; it demands an unwavering commitment to love – both for yourself and for others. This love, unyielding and profound, doesn't allow for the luxury of avoidance or negotiation. Instead, it compels us to confront our challenges head-on, to look deeply into the mirror of our experiences and see what truly lies within. It's a journey that calls for courage, for the strength to face not just the external manifestations of fear but its root in our own vulnerabilities and shadows.

Leading from love, we embark on a transformative process that begins with the self. This introspective voyage reveals that the antidote to fear and toxicity is not found in denial or retribution but in understanding, acceptance, and compassion. It is a realization that true leadership emanates from the heart, guided by a love that seeks to heal rather than to harm, to unite rather than to divide. In this space, love acts as a mirror, reflecting our essence and challenging us to embody the values we seek to inspire in others.

This path of confronting fear with love illuminates the interconnectedness of our emotional, intellectual, and spiritual selves. It underscores the importance of groundedness in navigating the complexities of human relationships, advocating for an approach to leadership that is empathetic, mindful, and grounded in love. This holistic perspective fosters an environment where individuals feel valued and understood, where their well-being is a priority, and where they are empowered to grow and thrive.

The principles of love and courage find resonance in the methodologies like sociocracy, which emphasize flexibility, collaboration, and shared governance. These approaches echo the sentiment that facing challenges with an open heart and a collaborative spirit can lead to innovative solutions and sustainable growth. It's a reminder that in business, as in life, the most resilient and dynamic communities are those built on the foundations of trust, respect, and mutual support.

When confronted with the shadows of fear and toxicity, love offers no escape but a path forward – a path that requires us to look deeply into the mirror of our actions and intentions, and to choose love over fear, compassion over indifference, and unity over division. It is a journey that not only transforms the individual but has the power to reshape organizations and societies, lighting the way to a future where love and courage triumph over fear and toxicity.

You have to keep breaking your heart until it opens.

In the pursuit of professional success and personal fulfillment, the journey is often marked by challenges that test our resolve, shake our confidence, and sometimes, break our hearts. These moments, though fraught with discomfort, are not mere obstacles; they are invitations to go deeper into the essence of who we are and what we truly value. It is through these trials that we are given the opportunity to transcend our limitations and discover a wellspring of resilience, compassion, and love within ourselves. This process of breaking and healing, of confronting our vulnerabilities and fears, paves the way for a profound transformation, both at work and in the broader scope of life.

Leading from love, we begin to approach our professional endeavors not as battles to be won, but as landscapes to be nurtured with care, empathy, and a deep-seated respect for the human spirit. This shift in perspective reveals that the true nature of work is not about enduring suffering but about engaging with our tasks and colleagues in a manner that is enriching, meaningful, and grounded in love. By opening ourselves to this perspective, we allow our hearts to guide us toward practices and relationships that honor our well-being and the well-being of those around us.

In this environment, the concepts of human-centered design become more than just abstract ideals; they are the very principles that shape our daily interactions and decisions. They encourage us to create spaces where vulnerability is met with support, where challenges are navigated with collective wisdom, and where each individual's growth is recognized as integral to the success of the whole. It is in these spaces that we discover the courage to show up authentically, to share our ideas and dreams, and to connect with others in ways that are both profound and transformative.

The journey toward opening our hearts in the workplace invites us to recognize the interconnectedness of our personal values and our professional goals. It challenges us to align our actions with our deeper purpose and to find harmony between what we do and who we aspire to be. This alignment fosters a sense of fulfillment that transcends external achievements, grounding us in a sense of purpose and joy that nourishes our souls.

The path to unlocking the full potential of our work and our lives lies in our willingness to continually break open our hearts, to embrace the lessons hidden within our struggles, and to allow love to be the guiding force in our journey. By doing so, we not only transform our own experience of work but also contribute to creating a world where compassion, resilience, and genuine connection are the hallmarks of success.

You think you are alive because you breathe air?

Shame on you, that you are alive in such a limited way.

Don't be without Love, so you won't feel dead.

Die in Love and stay alive forever.

In a world that often equates existence with the mere act of breathing, there lies a profound misconception about what it truly means to be alive. The essence of life extends far beyond the physical dimensions of air and breath; it is found in the depth of love, passion, and the relentless pursuit of beauty, joy, and growth. This perspective challenges us to redefine our understanding of vitality and to embrace a mode of living that transcends the ordinary.

Leading from love, we begin to see work not as an obligation or a means to an end but as a canvas for creative expression and personal development. The notion that people who merely live to work are experiencing a form of existential lethargy is a call to awaken to the possibilities that lie in engaging with our endeavors with enthusiasm and purpose. It suggests that true aliveness is achieved through the act of dying in love – with our dreams, our passions, and our projects – and in doing so, discovering a form of immortality through the legacy we create.

The transition from existing to truly living requires a shift from viewing work as a series of tasks to be completed to seeing it as an opportunity to contribute to something greater than ourselves. It involves fostering environments where simplicity and love are the foundations upon which we build our interactions and operations. These principles encourage us to approach our roles with a sense of innocence, curiosity, and openness, allowing for the emergence of innovative ideas and collaborative efforts that reflect our shared humanity and aspirations.

The integration of mindfulness within this framework is pivotal. It empowers individuals to navigate the complexities of professional and personal relationships with empathy, understanding, and respect. The cultivation of positive team dynamics ensures that every member of the organization feels valued, heard, and motivated to contribute their best, fostering a culture of continuous learning and mutual support.

The adoption of self-managing methods within this context is not merely about improving efficiency or organizational structure but about creating systems that are reflective of our intrinsic values and vision for a better world. These methodologies enable us to adapt and evolve in harmony with our environment and the needs of those we serve, ensuring that our work remains relevant, impactful, and aligned with our deepest convictions.

The journey toward redefining aliveness in the context of work and creation is a transformative process that invites us to immerse ourselves fully in the act of loving what we do and doing what we love. In doing so, we not only enrich our own lives but also contribute to a collective elevation of spirit, purpose, and joy, leaving a lasting imprint on the world that echoes through eternity.

choose love. choose love.

without this beautiful love,

life is nothing but a burden.

In a world often caught in the paradox of living to work and working to live, there emerges a beacon of hope for those yearning for a deeper meaning in their professional lives. This beacon, not visible to the eye but felt with the heart, illuminates a path that transcends the mundane cycle of daily tasks and targets. It whispers of a way of being, where the lines between personal fulfillment and professional achievement blur, merging into a harmonious existence that enriches both the individual and the collective.

Leading from love transforms this whispered possibility into a palpable reality. It elevates the act of leadership to an art form, where every decision, every interaction, and every goal is infused with a deeper purpose. This form of leadership is not about exerting control or asserting dominance but about nurturing, empowering, and inspiring. It's about creating an environment where people don't just come to work; they come to contribute to a cause they believe in, to be part of a community that values them, and to grow in ways they never thought possible.

The essence of this approach lies in recognizing that at the heart of every business endeavor, there's a human endeavor. It's about seeing beyond the spreadsheets and the strategies to the dreams, fears, and potential of the people who bring them to life. This vision demands a delicate balance, harmonizing the head's logic with the heart's empathy and the spirit's intuition. It requires leaders to be agile in their thinking, holistic in their approach, and resilient in their commitment to fostering an environment where trust flourishes and innovation thrives.

Such leadership does not shy away from the challenges and complexities of the modern business world. Instead, it embraces them as opportunities to demonstrate that principles and profits are not mutually exclusive but mutually reinforcing. It proves that when organizations operate from a place of love – valuing people over profits, well-being over wealth, and purpose over productivity – they not only achieve greater success but also contribute to a more just, sustainable, and compassionate world.

Leading from love redefines what it means to be successful. It's not just about the milestones reached or the accolades received but about the lives touched, the communities transformed, and the legacy left behind. It's a testament to the power of love to elevate our work and our lives, reminding us that when we choose love, we choose a life that is not just a burden to be borne but a gift to be cherished and shared. This is the heart of true leadership, where love is both the journey and the destination, guiding us to a future where work is not just a means to live but a way to bring more love into the world.

The deeper the grief, the more radiant the love.

Toxic and sociopathic people at work can be challenging, but they also offer us an opportunity to discover profound inner strength and love. When faced with negativity, it is easy to succumb to the same low vibrations. However, by viewing these interactions as invitations to grow, we can transform adversity into a source of empowerment.

Leading from love, we realize that our response to toxicity defines our character. Instead of reacting with anger or frustration, we can choose compassion and empathy. This does not mean accepting harmful behavior; rather, it means setting boundaries with kindness and maintaining our integrity. By staying true to our values, we create an environment where negativity cannot thrive.

Every challenging interaction teaches us something valuable about ourselves. It reveals our triggers, highlights our strengths, and shows us where we need to grow. Embracing these lessons with an open heart allows us to become more resilient and self-aware. We learn to stand firm in our truth, even when others try to shake our foundation.

One of the most powerful ways to counteract toxicity is through genuine acts of kindness. Simple gestures, like offering a listening ear or a word of encouragement, can have a profound impact. These acts not only uplift others but also reinforce our commitment to a positive, loving work environment.

In dealing with toxic individuals, it's essential to remain mindful of our own energy. Practices like mindfulness and meditation can help us stay centered and calm. By nurturing our inner peace, we become less susceptible to external negativity. This inner stability allows us to respond to challenges with grace and composure.

Creating a culture of love and respect at work starts with us. When we lead by example, we inspire others to follow suit. Our actions can influence the entire workplace, fostering a sense of unity and collaboration. This ripple effect can transform even the most toxic environments into spaces of growth and positivity.

It's also crucial to seek support when needed. Surround yourself with like-minded individuals who uplift and inspire you. A strong support network can provide the encouragement and perspective needed to navigate difficult situations. Together, you can create a collective force for positive change.

Leading from love means recognizing the humanity in everyone, even those who seem unlovable. By approaching each interaction with compassion, we tap into a wellspring of inner power. This power not only helps us navigate toxic environments but also illuminates our path forward.

Love said to me, there is nothing that is not me. Be silent.

In the rich flow of life and work, the pursuit of perfection often becomes an elusive goal, shadowed by the inevitable presence of imperfections. Yet, it is within this contrast – the interplay between what we deem perfect and imperfect – that the true essence of love and beauty emerges. This realization invites us to embrace the entirety of our experiences, recognizing that the very contrasts we encounter are not obstacles to love and beauty but are integral to their existence.

Leading from love, we are encouraged to view our professional endeavors and personal journeys not as quests for unattainable flawlessness but as opportunities to find harmony within the contrasts. This perspective illuminates the richness of our experiences, teaching us that every challenge, every setback, and every triumph is imbued with love and beauty, waiting to be acknowledged and embraced.

The application of this understanding extends beyond the philosophical, influencing how we engage with our work, our colleagues, and the missions of our organizations. It prompts us to incorporate practices that value simplicity, authenticity, and a profound respect for the diversity of experiences and perspectives. By doing so, we cultivate environments where care and respect flourish, enabling us to respond to challenges with empathy, creativity, and resilience.

The principles of participative organizational structures provide a framework for navigating the contrasts inherent in our work. These methodologies encourage us to remain adaptable, to seek out and celebrate the contributions of every individual, and to recognize that the collective wisdom of a team is amplified when it embraces a spectrum of experiences and viewpoints.

The journey toward embracing the contrasts in our lives and work is a journey of discovering the omnipresence of love and beauty. It is a call to silence our inner critics and to listen with open hearts to the lessons that imperfections teach us about strength, growth, and the boundless capacity for love. This journey transforms our understanding of perfection, revealing that it is not the absence of imperfection but the acceptance and integration of it that leads to true fulfillment and beauty.

As we move forward, let us carry with us the wisdom that love encompasses all – both the light and the shadows, the peaks and the valleys. By honoring the contrasts, we open ourselves to a deeper appreciation of life's complexity and the myriad ways in which love manifests around us and within us, guiding us toward a more compassionate, inclusive, and vibrant way of living and working.

Go find yourself first so you can also find me.

A leader of others must first be a leader of themselves. This profound truth underscores the importance of self-discovery and personal growth as the foundation of effective leadership. Before one can guide others, they must first navigate their own inner landscape, finding clarity, purpose, and strength within.

Leading from love involves embarking on this journey of self-leadership with humility and an open heart. It means acknowledging our own limitations and continuously striving for personal betterment. By cultivating a deep understanding of ourselves, we can lead others with authenticity, empathy, and wisdom.

In the context of leadership, this approach fosters a culture of trust and transparency. When leaders are true to themselves and their principles, they inspire others to do the same. This authenticity creates a strong foundation for meaningful connections and effective collaboration. It encourages team members to bring their whole selves to work, contributing to a more cohesive and dynamic organization.

Engaging with the concept of self-leadership also involves setting clear intentions and maintaining a focused mindset. It means prioritizing actions that align with our core values and letting go of those that do not serve our higher purpose. This disciplined approach ensures that our leadership is guided by integrity and a commitment to the greater good.

This journey of self-discovery and self-leadership is not a solitary endeavor. It requires the support and encouragement of others who share our vision and values. By surrounding ourselves with like-minded individuals, we create a community that fosters growth and mutual respect. This collective energy amplifies our efforts, enabling us to achieve greater heights together.

Becoming a leader of ourselves is an ongoing process of reflection, learning, and growth. It demands that we remain open to new experiences and insights, continually evolving in our understanding of ourselves and the world around us. This path, guided by love, transforms us into leaders who are not only effective but also deeply connected to those we serve.

As we navigate this journey, we discover that true leadership begins within. By leading ourselves with clarity and purpose, we can lead others with compassion and vision. This alignment between inner and outer leadership creates a ripple effect, inspiring positive change and fostering a culture of authenticity and empowerment.

Both light and shadow are the dance of Love.

There is no possibility to experience joy and happiness without having experienced pain and grief, and the same is true for work where success is linked to failure.

Leading from love means understanding that the full spectrum of human experience, including both triumphs and setbacks, is essential to growth and fulfillment. It is through facing and embracing challenges that we come to appreciate our achievements fully. Love teaches us to see failure not as an endpoint but as a stepping stone to success.

This mindset transforms how we approach both personal and professional challenges. When we lead with love, we create a culture that supports and uplifts during times of difficulty, understanding that these moments are crucial for development. This environment not only helps individuals bounce back from setbacks but also encourages them to take risks and innovate, knowing that failure is part of the journey to success.

Recognizing that both joy and sorrow are integral to the dance of life allows us to lead with empathy and compassion. We become more attuned to the emotional landscapes of those we work with, offering support and encouragement when needed. This approach fosters deeper connections and a sense of community, where everyone feels valued and understood.

Creating an environment where authentic care and respect are prioritized allows people to express their true selves, including their fears and failures. When people feel safe, they are more likely to collaborate openly and creatively, which is essential for fostering innovation and driving the organization forward.

In practical terms, this means creating structures and practices that support positive reinforcement and continuous learning. Iterative progress and regular reflection help teams learn from each cycle and improve continuously, aligning perfectly with the idea that both success and failure are necessary for growth.

Understanding that light and shadow coexist in the dance of love enriches our leadership and our lives. It allows us to embrace the full range of experiences, learning from each and growing stronger. This holistic approach not only enhances our personal resilience but also builds a more robust and dynamic organization.

As we lead from love, we create a workplace where every experience, whether perceived as good or bad, contributes to the collective strength and wisdom of the team. This journey, enriched by both light and shadow, leads to a future where success is defined by our ability to learn, adapt, and thrive together.

You dance inside my chest where no one sees you.

In the silent corridors of our minds, there thrives a dance of passion, a silent ballet that often remains unseen by the world. This hidden choreography, vibrant with dreams and aspirations, pulses within us, urging us to reach beyond the mundane, to tap into the extraordinary. It's a melody of the soul, a rhythm of ideas and innovations that long to leap into the light. Yet, too often, we hold back, cocooned in our comfort zones, letting the fear of exposure mute the music that seeks to resonate beyond the confines of our hearts.

Leading from love, we start to understand that the most profound changes occur not just through the strength of our arguments or the brilliance of our strategies, but through the authenticity and vulnerability with which we present our ideas. It's about allowing the essence of who we are and what we believe to guide our steps, nurturing an environment where the unseen can flourish into the seen. It's about embodying a leadership style that invites collaboration, where each voice, no matter how soft, finds a listening ear, and every idea, regardless of its origin, receives the sunlight it needs to grow.

Imagine a world where we approach our interactions with the simplicity of a child's innocence, where our decisions are made through the lens of love, not fear. Picture a workplace that adapts as gracefully as nature does, embracing change with the flexibility of a reed in the wind. Here, creativity is not just encouraged but celebrated, and failure is seen not as a setback but as a step forward.

This vision is not just a distant dream but a reality that can be crafted through the collective efforts of individuals who dare to share their inner dances with the world. By fostering a culture of psychological openness, where people feel safe to express their true selves, we unlock the doors to unprecedented innovation and creativity. It's about designing systems and processes that are as human as the people they serve, recognizing that at the heart of every technological advance, every strategic pivot, there lies a human emotion, a personal dream.

As we align our actions with the magnetic pull of our deepest desires, we begin to attract opportunities that resonate with the essence of who we are. It becomes clear that the path to fulfillment and success is not found in conforming to the external, but in embracing the internal, in letting the dance within guide our steps. This is the journey of transformation, from the invisible to the visible, from the individual to the collective, where every heart beats in unison to the rhythm of shared dreams and aspirations.

This is a subtle truth. Whatever you love you are.

The essence of our being is intricately tied to the passions that ignite our spirit and the vocations that call to our hearts. This profound connection between what we love and who we are forms the bedrock of our authentic selves, a truth that invites us to reflect deeply on the nature of our professional and personal pursuits.

Leading from love, we embark on a journey to discover the core of our true self, finding that our deepest passions are not arbitrary or superficial. Instead, they are the purest expressions of our identity, the songs our souls sing when we engage in work that resonates with our innermost values and desires. This realization challenges us to look beyond societal expectations and conventional definitions of success, urging us to align our vocational choices with what genuinely brings us joy, fulfillment, and a sense of purpose.

In embracing this alignment, we are called to cultivate simplicity in our approach to work and life. By stripping away the complexities that often distract and detract from our core passions, we create space for love and innocence to flourish. This simplicity enables us to connect more deeply with the essence of our work, transforming daily tasks into expressions of our true selves.

The integration of leading from love into this paradigm is essential. It empowers us to navigate the rich spectrum of human emotions with empathy, compassion, and understanding, enhancing our connections with colleagues, customers, and the broader community. These connections are strengthened by our commitment to authenticity, as we lead with transparency and vulnerability, fostering environments of inclusiveness where everyone is encouraged to bring their whole selves to work.

The principles of self-managing teams and participative governance offer practical frameworks for realizing this vision within organizational structures. These methodologies prioritize flexibility, collaboration, and shared leadership, reflecting a collective commitment to work that is not only effective but deeply meaningful. They embody the belief that when individuals are free to pursue their passions within the context of their work, they unleash a powerful force for innovation, creativity, and positive change.

The journey towards aligning our vocations with our passions is a journey towards self-discovery and authenticity. It challenges us to redefine success, not as a destination but as a way of being, rooted in love, passion, and the relentless pursuit of what makes us come alive. By choosing to embrace our true selves in our work, we not only enrich our own lives but also contribute to a world where work is an expression of love, beauty, and the boundless potential of the human spirit.

Sit with lovers and choose their state.

Do not stay long with those who are not

living in the heart.

In the vast expanse of our professional journeys, the company we keep can illuminate or obscure the path we tread. The essence of our interactions, the quality of our engagements, speaks volumes not only about our present state but also about the trajectory of our future. It's in the power of connection, in the resonance of shared values and visions, that we find the catalyst for true innovation and transformation. The discernment to recognize those who embody a spirit of generosity, who live by the principles of kindness and compassion, becomes our guiding star. Aligning ourselves with individuals who radiate positivity, who navigate their lives and careers from a place of love rather than fear, is akin to choosing a path lit by the dawn's first light.

Leading from love, we understand that the environment we cultivate around us directly influences our inner peace and, by extension, our capacity for impactful leadership. It's in the serenity of our own hearts that we can best discern the energy of others, identifying those who share our commitment to building something greater than ourselves. This alignment of purpose and passion fosters a culture of mutual support and respect, where the exchange of ideas is not just encouraged but celebrated. It's an acknowledgment that the most profound growth occurs in the presence of those who not only dream of a better world but take tangible steps towards creating it

Imagine a workplace where every interaction is infused with this consciousness, where teams are built not just on the basis of skill but on the harmony of their members' hearts. In such a place, the simplicity of our shared human experience becomes the foundation for complex problem-solving and creativity. Here, the innocence of believing in the good, in the potential of each individual and idea, propels us towards our collective goals. This environment thrives on the balance between logical rigor and human awareness, between the ambition to innovate and the wisdom to do so with ethical integrity.

In this context, the principles of agility, collaboration, and positive psychology are not merely methodologies but expressions of a deeper understanding of human potential. They serve as reminders that the essence of our success lies not in the metrics we achieve but in the lives we touch and the legacy we leave. By choosing to surround ourselves with those who live from the heart, we not only elevate our own spirits but also become beacons of light in the lives of others.

This deliberate choice to connect with and learn from those who embody love in their actions and attitudes invites a profound transformation. It encourages us to not only aspire to greatness in our endeavors but to anchor our aspirations in the values that make life truly worth living.

If you want the moon, do not hide from the night.

If you want a rose, do not hide from the thorns.

If you want love, do not hide from yourself.

In the fabric of our professional lives, the pursuit of meaningful success often leads us through a labyrinth of challenges, each with its own set of thorns. Yet, it is precisely through navigating these challenges that we sketch the story of our most profound accomplishments. To strive for greatness in our work, to truly express the depth of our passion and commitment, we must be willing to embrace every aspect of the journey. This includes the tension and conflict that inevitably arise when we push against the boundaries of what's known, when we dare to innovate, to dream, and to lead with authenticity.

Leading from love, we come to understand that the essence of our work and the essence of ourselves are not separate entities but reflections of one another. Embracing the tensions that surface, viewing them not as obstacles but as opportunities for growth and understanding, allows us to deepen our connection to our work and to those with whom we share our journey. It's in this space that we find the courage to confront our own limitations, to challenge our assumptions, and to grow beyond what we previously thought possible. This approach transforms potential conflict into a catalyst for innovation, fostering an environment where diversity of thought and expression is not just tolerated but celebrated.

Imagine a workplace that thrives on this philosophy, where every individual is encouraged to bring their whole selves to their roles, where the nuances of each person's uniqueness are seen as invaluable assets. In such a place, the simplicity of shared goals unites the energy of the diverse talents and perspectives, creating a collective strength that is both resilient and adaptive. Here, the balance between achieving ambitious targets and maintaining a nurturing, inclusive culture is gracefully maintained, guided by leaders who recognize that the true measure of success is found not in the absence of conflict but in the ability to engage with it constructively.

In this environment, the principles of adaptability, collaboration, and mutual respect are not just operational strategies but expressions of a deeper commitment to creating a workplace that mirrors the best aspects of humanity. It's a setting where the challenges we face, both internally and externally, are not roadblocks but stepping stones, leading us toward greater understanding, innovation, and connection.

By embracing the full spectrum of our experiences, by not shying away from the night or the thorns, we allow ourselves to discover the full moon of our potential and the blooming rose of our endeavors. This is the path to finding not just success but fulfillment in our work, to expressing love through our actions and our choices, and ultimately, to finding ourselves in the work we do.

whenever we manage to love without expectations, calculations, negotiations, we are indeed in heaven.

In our bustling professional lives, where ambitions soar and competition thrives, there exists a profound, yet often overlooked, truth. The essence of true fulfillment in our work does not lie in the accumulation of personal gains or recognition but in the sheer joy of creating value for others without any strings attached. This selfless approach to our endeavors not only elevates our spirit but also transforms our workplace into a sanctuary of innovation and collaboration. When we dedicate ourselves to the service of others, pouring our passion into projects and people without the shadow of personal agendas, we experience a form of liberation that is as rare as it is exhilarating.

Leading from love, we embark on a journey that transcends the traditional metrics of success. It's a path less traveled, where the measure of our accomplishments is not quantified by what we receive but by the impact we make. In this paradigm, our work becomes a reflection of our deepest values, a manifestation of our desire to contribute, to uplift, and to inspire. This ethos fosters an environment where the collective goal transcends individual ambition, where the success of one is celebrated as the success of all. It's in this spirit of unconditional giving that we discover the most authentic expression of ourselves and the true meaning of freedom at work.

Imagine a workplace where this philosophy permeates every interaction, every project, every strategy. It's a place where simplicity guides complexity, where the clarity of purpose and purity of intention shine through in every endeavor. Here, the intricate dance of balancing logic with empathy, ambition with humility, and innovation with compassion creates an ecosystem that thrives on mutual respect and genuine care. Such an environment not only nurtures emotional and intellectual growth but also cultivates a deep sense of belonging and purpose among its members.

This approach to work, rooted in the act of giving without expectation, ignites a powerful transformation. It turns the workplace into a space for personal and collective evolution, where the barriers between the professional and the personal begin to blur, revealing a canvas where every individual has the opportunity to paint with the vibrant colors of their unique talents and passions.

By fostering this culture of selfless passion and unconditional contribution, we unlock a level of creativity, satisfaction, and achievement that traditional paradigms cannot offer. It's a state of being where every moment at work is an opportunity to touch lives, to make a difference, and to experience the joy of being part of something greater than ourselves. This, in its essence, is the heaven we create not just for ourselves but for everyone around us, a testament to the transformative power of love in action.

Becoming 'Awake' involves seeing our confusion more clearly.

In the bustling world of work, where deadlines loom and targets constantly shift, there's a profound, often overlooked truth about happiness. It doesn't spring from a relentless pursuit of perfection or a meticulously controlled environment. Rather, true joy and fulfillment at work emerge when we embrace the reality of uncertainties and unknowns, recognizing them not as threats but as opportunities for growth, creativity, and connection. The journey towards awakening in our professional lives begins the moment we acknowledge our confusions, our imperfections, and the beautiful chaos of the world around us, seeing them through a lens of clarity and acceptance.

Leading from love, we understand that the essence of a fulfilling work life is not found in eliminating challenges but in engaging with them more deeply, in recognizing the inherent beauty and potential in the unknown. It's in this engagement that we find the courage to innovate, to take risks, and to stand by our values, even when the path ahead is shrouded in fog. This approach fosters a culture of resilience, where each member of the team is empowered to bring their whole selves to their roles, embracing their vulnerabilities as sources of strength.

Imagine a workplace that thrives on this philosophy, where the unknown is greeted not with fear but with curiosity and excitement. In such a place, the simplicity of our shared human experience becomes a guiding star, illuminating the way through the complexities of business challenges. Here, the innocence of exploration and discovery infuses daily tasks with meaning and joy, while the harmony between our emotional, intellectual, and spiritual selves cultivates a deep sense of belonging and purpose.

This environment is not just a figment of imagination but a real possibility when we choose to lead and work from a place of love and acceptance. It's a setting where agility and innovation are natural byproducts of a culture that values the unpredictable journey over the destination, where leading from love is the foundation upon which we build our collective success.

By embracing the uncertainties and confusions of our work with an open heart and a clear mind, we unlock a new dimension of professional happiness. It's a state of being that transcends the superficial markers of success, offering instead a sense of fulfillment that is deeply rooted in the authenticity and growth of each individual. In this awakened state, we not only navigate the complexities of our work with grace and resilience but also contribute to a world where the beautiful unknowns are celebrated as gateways to innovation, connection, and true happiness.

Appear as you are.

Be as you appear.

In the bustling hallways of modern business, where innovation races against the clock and communication flows faster than thought, there exists a timeless principle that shapes the foundation of true success. It's the essence of showing up, not just as a title or a role, but as the entirety of who you are. In this world, your most significant advantage is the authenticity you bring to the table every day. It's about shedding the layers of pretense and embracing the power of being genuinely you.

Leading from love, the journey begins. In an environment where strategies and systems evolve at a breakneck pace, the core of impactful leadership remains unchanged: the courage to present one's true self. This approach is not just about emotional expression. It is a harmonious blend of mind, heart, and spirit. It's about fostering an environment where voices are heard, ideas are respected, and the individuality of each team member is celebrated. Here, success is measured not only by outcomes but by the authenticity and passion that drive them.

Imagine a workspace where simplicity is the backbone of complexity, where the pursuit of innovation is grounded in the fundamental truths of our human experience. Here, every project, every meeting, and every strategy is infused with the essence of who we are at our core. This is not about discarding professional rigor. It is about enhancing it with a touch of humanity, making every decision, every achievement more meaningful and connected to a larger purpose.

This approach transcends traditional business models, fostering an agile environment where growth is not just a target but a journey of continuous learning and adaptation. It's a culture that values the individual but thrives on collaboration, where the strength of the team is amplified by the unique contribution of each member. This is a place where leadership is not a position but an action, guided by the innate understanding that to inspire others, one must first be true to yourself.

In this mode, the magnetic pull of authenticity attracts opportunities, relationships, and successes that resonate with the genuine essence of our being. It's where our true potential unfolds, not because we seek to fulfill external expectations, but because we are aligned with our innermost values and intentions. This alignment brings about a profound transformation, not just in how we work, but in how we perceive the world around us.

Thus, in the grand tapestry of business, where different threads of thought, strategy, and innovation intertwine, the most vibrant colors come from the threads that are true to their hue. It's a reminder that in the pursuit of success, the most powerful tool we have is the authenticity we bring to every moment, every challenge, and every opportunity.

The more awake one is to the material world,

the more one is asleep to spirit.

In the relentless pursuit of success, it's easy to become ensnared by the tangible rewards of our labor – the promotions, the paychecks, the prestige. These are often seen as the yardsticks of professional achievement, the benchmarks that separate the successful from the rest. Yet, in this endless chase for material gain, there's a risk of overlooking something far more essential – the joy and satisfaction derived not from what our work gives us, but from what it awakens within us. The true measure of success, then, might not be in the wealth accumulated but in the fulfillment found and the lives touched along the way.

Leading from love, the narrative shifts from one of accumulation to one of contribution and purpose. It's a journey where the value of our work is not quantified by external accolades but by the internal satisfaction it brings. It's about finding meaning in the challenges we overcome, the connections we forge, and the growth we experience. This path champions the idea that our professional endeavors should not only advance our careers but also enrich our spirits and ignite our passions.

By refocusing our aspirations, we cultivate a workplace that thrives on more than just efficiency and outcomes. We foster environments where creativity and innovation are born from a place of genuine enthusiasm and where tasks are infused with a sense of purpose. In such spaces, the pursuit of excellence is motivated by a deeper calling, not just the bottom line. This holistic approach to work cultivates not only a more satisfying professional life but a more balanced and fulfilling personal life as well.

The quest for material success can often overshadow the profound joy found in the simple moments – the laughter shared with colleagues, the satisfaction of a job well done, the thrill of learning something new. These are the experiences that breathe life into our daily routines, transforming them from mundane tasks into sources of joy and inspiration. When we shift our focus from living to work to working to live, every moment becomes an opportunity to find deeper satisfaction and meaning.

Embracing this philosophy does not mean shunning ambition or eschewing success. Instead, it's about redefining what success means to us. It's about balancing our drive for achievement with our need for fulfillment, ensuring that as we climb the ladder of success, we remain grounded in the values that give our work meaning. In doing so, we don't just achieve success; we redefine it, discovering that true satisfaction comes not from what we acquire but from what we contribute and how we grow. This is the journey to finding joy in our work, a path that leads not just to greater success but to a richer, more meaningful life.

My soul is from elsewhere, I'm sure of that,

and I intend to end up there.

In the grand scheme of our professional journeys, amidst the relentless pursuit of success, achievements, and recognition, it's crucial to remember the impermanent nature of these conquests. We arrive in this world without titles, possessions, or accolades, and it is in that same state that we will one day depart. Yet, this realization isn't a call to nihilism but an invitation to align our endeavors with a deeper understanding of our existence and purpose beyond the physical world. This perspective invites us to consider not just what we are working towards but why, urging us to infuse our careers with meaning that transcends material success.

Leading from love, we begin to navigate our careers not just as a path to personal gain but as a journey towards something greater. This approach does not diminish ambition; rather, it elevates it, grounding our aspirations in the pursuit of contributions that extend beyond ourselves. It encourages us to view success not as an end goal but as a byproduct of our commitment to making a positive impact in the lives of others and in the world at large. In this light, each achievement becomes a milestone not just in our professional development but in our spiritual and emotional evolution as well.

Embracing this broader perspective transforms the workplace into a place of opportunity for personal and collective growth. It fosters an environment where innovation is driven by a desire to serve, where leadership is characterized by empathy and integrity, and where challenges are met with resilience and a deep-seated belief in the potential for positive change. In such a culture, the emphasis shifts from competing to contributing, from achieving for the sake of status to achieving for the sake of impact.

This paradigm invites us to consider our legacy, to ponder how our actions and decisions will resonate beyond the immediate context of our work. It's a reminder that the true value of our professional endeavors lies not in the wealth they generate or the recognition they garner but in the difference they make. It challenges us to live and work in a way that, when we look back, we can see a trail of meaningful contributions, relationships built on genuine connections, and a consistent effort to reach beyond the material towards something more enduring.

In adopting this mindset, we anchor our careers in a sense of purpose that guides us through the ebbs and flows of professional life. It helps us maintain perspective during times of triumph and adversity alike, reminding us that our true essence and destination lie beyond the tangible achievements of our work. By keeping this perspective at the forefront of our minds, we cultivate a career that not only fulfills us on a material level but enriches us on a spiritual and emotional one, aligning our professional journey with the greater journey of our lives.

Doing as others told me, I was blind.

Coming when others called me, I was lost.

Then I left everyone, myself as well.

Then I found myself, myself as well.

Leading from love means embracing your true self and understanding that only through authenticity are you able to create the magic you desire at work. Often, we are told not to be selfish, to conform to the demands of others, and to put their needs before our own. But when others ask us to abandon our desires to serve theirs, they are being selfish themselves. True success and fulfillment come from listening to your inner voice and pursuing your unique path.

At work, this means recognizing that your creativity, passion, and individuality are your greatest assets. When you suppress these qualities to fit into someone else's mold, you not only diminish your potential but also contribute less authentically to the team. It is through your distinct perspective and approach that innovation thrives. By being true to yourself, you bring a richness and diversity to the workplace that cannot be replicated by mere conformity.

Being selfish in this context is not about disregarding others' needs; it is about honoring your own so that you can contribute more fully and passionately. When you are aligned with your true self, your work becomes more than a task; it becomes a reflection of your inner creativity and purpose. This alignment fosters a sense of fulfillment and joy that radiates outwards, positively affecting those around you.

Consider the times when you have felt most alive and engaged at work. Likely, these were moments when you were allowed to express your unique talents and ideas freely. This is the essence of leading from love – creating an environment where everyone feels empowered to bring their whole selves to the table. Such an environment not only enhances individual satisfaction but also drives collective success.

When you lead from love, you inspire others to do the same. Your authenticity becomes a beacon, encouraging your colleagues to embrace their own truths. This creates a culture of mutual respect and admiration, where everyone feels valued for who they are. It is in this space of shared authenticity that true collaboration and innovation occur.

Moreover, embracing your individuality does not mean working in isolation. It means bringing your full self into the collaborative process, contributing your unique insights while remaining open to the perspectives of others. This dynamic interplay of individuality and collaboration is where the magic happens. By staying true to yourself, you create a ripple effect that transforms the workplace into a vibrant, creative, and supportive community.

Set your life on fire.

Seek those who fan the flames.

In professional life, the most luminous threads are those colored by passion and purpose. The journey to find and nurture this brilliance within ourselves often leads us through various landscapes, some barren, others rich in opportunity and inspiration. The quest, however, is not just about discovering what sets our souls ablaze but also about surrounding ourselves with environments and communities that cherish and fuel this inner fire. It's a pursuit that calls for courage, for the willingness to venture beyond the familiar, seeking places where our talents are not just recognized but ardently encouraged.

Leading from love, we recognize the transformative power of working within organizations that resonate with our deepest values and aspirations. These are the spaces where creativity is not just welcomed but celebrated, where innovation is the norm rather than the exception. In such environments, our work becomes more than a means to an end; it evolves into a reflection of our essence, a manifestation of what truly energizes us from within. This alignment between our inner world and our external endeavors creates a powerful synergy, propelling us toward unparalleled heights of achievement and fulfillment.

This journey is also a testament to the importance of emotional intelligence in the workplace. The ability to understand and manage our emotions, and to empathize with those of others, becomes the bridge that connects us with like-minded individuals. These connections, based on mutual respect and understanding, form the foundation of teams that not only excel but also support each member's personal growth and well-being. It is within these dynamic collectives that we find the encouragement to push boundaries, to innovate, and to continually seek ways to bring our best selves to our work.

Moreover, the concept of psychological safety plays a critical role in nurturing the flames of passion and purpose. In an environment where taking risks is encouraged and failure is seen as a stepping stone to learning, our inner fire finds the oxygen it needs to burn brighter. This culture of trust and openness fosters a sense of belonging, where every individual feels empowered to contribute their unique ideas and perspectives, knowing that their contributions are valued and respected.

In essence, the path to professional fulfillment and personal growth is lit by the flames of our own passion and the support of those who fan them. It's a journey that requires us to seek out and cultivate environments that not only acknowledge our unique talents but also provide the space, tools, and inspiration necessary to bring our visions to life. By aligning ourselves with organizations and communities that resonate with our core values and aspirations, we set the stage for a life of purpose, achievement, and joy, embodying the true essence of creating a legacy that reflects the brightest versions of ourselves.

If all you can do is crawl, start crawling.

Every master started out unknowing anything about the topic of their passion and expertise. If your intuition is driving you towards mastery, simply start on the journey in the way you can. The first steps are often the most challenging, but they are also the most crucial. These initial movements set the stage for a journey filled with growth, discovery, and eventual mastery.

Leading from love means embracing the humble beginnings of your journey. It acknowledges that the path to greatness is often marked by small, seemingly insignificant steps. These steps, however, are imbued with the power of intention and the promise of transformation. Each crawl forward is a testament to your commitment to your vision and your willingness to pursue it despite uncertainties and challenges.

In the context of business, this philosophy encourages a culture of perseverance and resilience. When leaders adopt the mindset of starting where they are, they inspire their teams to do the same. This approach fosters an environment where progress is valued over perfection, and where every effort, no matter how small, is seen as a vital contribution to the overall goal. It shifts the focus from immediate results to sustained growth and continuous improvement.

Moreover, this journey requires a deep connection to one's intuition. Trusting your inner guidance allows you to navigate the unknown with confidence and clarity. It empowers you to make decisions that align with your true purpose and to move forward with a sense of assurance, even when the path ahead is unclear. This trust in your intuition is a cornerstone of effective leadership, as it enables you to lead with authenticity and conviction.

Leading from love also means nurturing your spirit and intuition as you progress. It involves creating a balance between pushing forward and allowing yourself the space to reflect and recharge. This balance is essential for maintaining the energy and enthusiasm needed to pursue long-term goals. By taking care of your inner self, you ensure that you can continue to lead with passion and purpose.

As you embark on this journey, remember that every master was once a beginner. Embrace the early stages of your path with gratitude and determination. Celebrate the small victories and learn from the setbacks. Each step, no matter how small, brings you closer to your goal and strengthens your resolve.

The journey to mastery is a continuous process of learning and evolving. Trust in your intuition, embrace the humble beginnings, and lead with love and intention. As you move forward, you will find that each crawl, each step, and each leap brings you closer to realizing your fullest potential. This journey, guided by love and fueled by determination, is what transforms aspirations into achievements and dreams into reality.

Insights for Leading Strategy & Innovation

Run from what's comfortable.

Forget safety.

Live where you fear to live.

Destroy your reputation.

Be notorious.

Daring to become a truly sustainable company despite the cost and risk requires a radical shift in mindset and action. It means stepping away from the comfortable and predictable, embracing the unknown, and committing to a path that challenges the status quo. This journey is not for the faint-hearted but for those who see the profound potential in aligning their business practices with the principles of sustainability.

Leading from love means infusing every decision and action with a deep sense of care and commitment to the planet and future generations. It's about recognizing that true sustainability goes beyond environmental impact; it encompasses a holistic approach that includes social and economic dimensions. This kind of leadership demands courage, resilience, and an unwavering belief in the greater good.

This commitment to simplicity and sustainability requires balancing emotional, intellectual, and spiritual aspects of the business. Emotionally, it involves fostering a culture where employees feel connected to the mission and motivated to contribute to positive change. Intellectually, it means staying informed and innovative, continuously seeking new ways to reduce the ecological footprint and enhance social value. Spiritually, it involves cultivating a sense of purpose and connection to something larger than yourself.

The path to sustainability is fraught with challenges, but it also offers immense rewards. By daring to take bold steps, companies can lead by example, inspiring others to follow suit. This journey is not just about compliance or public image. It is about creating a legacy of positive impact that transcends generations.

Embracing this journey also means accepting the inherent risks and uncertainties. It requires a willingness to invest in long-term gains over short-term profits and to view setbacks as opportunities for growth and learning. It's about fostering an environment of openness where innovation and experimentation are encouraged, and where failure is seen as a stepping stone to success.

By leading from love and embracing simplicity, companies can navigate the complexities of sustainability with grace and determination. This approach not only benefits the environment but also enhances the overall well-being of employees, communities, and stakeholders. It creates a ripple effect, spreading positive change far and wide.

Daring to become a truly sustainable company is an act of love and courage. It's a commitment to doing what is right, even when it's difficult. It's about leaving a lasting legacy that future generations will thank you for, and about living in alignment with the highest values and ideals.

Let the beauty of what you love be what you do.

The creation of a product is not just a process – it's an art form where passion and purpose converge. It is a pursuit that goes beyond mere functionality or profitability; it is a craft honed with a deep-seated affection for those who will ultimately use what is created. When the essence of this affection is woven into the vision, strategy, and roadmap of a product, it transcends the ordinary, becoming something that not only serves a need but also delights and connects with the user on a profound level.

Leading from love, product visionaries are those rare individuals who can glimpse the world through the eyes of their customers, feeling their needs as their own. This empathetic approach is the heartbeat of innovation, guiding the hands and minds of those who build not just with intelligence but with care. It is not enough to predict what users might need; the goal is to understand what will enrich their lives, what will resonate with their innermost desires, and what will serve them not just efficiently, but meaningfully.

This ethos permeates every layer of product development. It is evident in the simplicity of a design that users intuitively navigate, in the reliability that earns their trust, and in the joy they experience with each interaction. Such a product becomes more than a tool; it becomes a companion on the user's journey, reflecting a commitment to their satisfaction and well-being. This alignment between a product's purpose and the user's needs is the hallmark of a strategy rooted in genuine care.

When a roadmap unfolds from this foundation, it charts a course not of features and functions alone but of experiences and emotions. It anticipates not only market trends but human reactions, fostering a connection that is less about transactions and more about relationships. It's a roadmap that evolves, not at the whims of technology alone but in harmony with the evolving human story.

In crafting a product with this level of dedication, a team must embrace flexibility and collaboration, hallmarks of methodologies that value people over processes. They must foster an environment where learning and discovery is paramount, where ideas are shared freely, and creativity flourishes. The journey of creating such a product is not without challenges, but it is filled with the satisfaction that comes from knowing that every decision, every line of code, every design element was infused with affection and care.

When a product is a reflection of this kind of love, it does more than succeed in the market – it resonates in the hearts of those who use it, becoming a small, yet integral part of their lives. This resonance is the true reward for those who choose to infuse their work with love, creating not just a product but a legacy of care.

when you feel a peaceful joy,

that's when you are near truth.

The crossroads of decision-making in business are often clouded with the fog of data, opinions, and forecasts. Yet, beneath the layers of complexity, there's a compass that often points to the truth – a serene inner voice, an intuitive whisper. This inner guidance, when heeded, cuts through the noise and directs leaders to choices that resonate with the core of their values and the heart of their vision. It's an emotional and spiritual alignment that, when reached, confirms the soundness of a decision beyond the black and white of spreadsheets and analytics.

Leading from love, the approach to strategy shifts from one of mere logic to one of holistic wisdom. This is not to suggest that data and rationality do not have their places – they are the maps and instruments that guide the ship – but intuition is the steady hand on the tiller, feeling the wind and the waves, sensing the right course through experience, empathy, and insight. It is this balance that allows leaders to navigate the often tumultuous waters of business strategy with a sense of peace and purpose.

Such decisions, made from a place of inner calm and clarity, have the power to transform not just companies but the lives of the people within them. They foster environments where teams feel secure and valued, where the safe space to express ideas and concerns is the norm, and where the collective spirit is nurtured by the knowledge that their leaders are acting with authenticity and heart. This environment is the fertile ground in which innovation and creativity thrive, where agile responses to change are made not in fear but in confidence.

A strategy born of this intuitive process is more than a set of directives; it is a narrative that people can believe in and rally behind. It is a story that speaks not just to the minds of employees, customers, and stakeholders but to their spirits. This kind of strategy doesn't just direct; it inspires, aligns, and unites.

The true measure of strategic decisions lies not in their immediate outcomes but in the sustained harmony they create – the peaceful joy that signifies not just a good choice but the right path. This is the essence of a vision brought to life by leaders who understand that the best decisions are those made by integrating all facets of wisdom: the intellectual, the emotional, and the intuitive. It's a holistic approach that acknowledges the complexity of business but also the profound simplicity of truth, guiding the way to a future where success is not just achieved but felt and lived.

Reason is powerless in the expression of Love.

Creating for the sake of beauty and truth transforms the way we approach business and life. This deeper understanding allows us to move past mere logic and embrace the essence of what it means to create something truly meaningful. In this space, love and intuition guide our actions, leading to outcomes that resonate on a profound level.

Leading from love means recognizing that some of the most impactful decisions come from the heart, not the mind. It's about trusting that the pursuit of beauty and truth can drive innovation and excellence in ways that pure rationality cannot. This approach allows us to tap into a wellspring of creativity and passion, inspiring us to go beyond conventional boundaries and explore new possibilities.

Simplicity is the key idea that underpins this philosophy. By focusing on the purest and most essential aspects of our work, we strip away unnecessary complexities and connect with our true purpose. Simplicity allows us to see clearly, act decisively, and create with authenticity. It is through this lens that we can bring beauty and truth to the forefront of our endeavors.

In practice, this means fostering an environment where respect and care are prioritized. When team members feel valued and understood, they are more likely to take risks, share bold ideas, and contribute to a culture of innovation. This safe space encourages the kind of creativity that leads to extraordinary outcomes, as individuals feel free to express their true selves and explore uncharted territories.

Balancing emotional, intellectual, and spiritual elements in decision-making enriches the process, ensuring that our actions are aligned with our deepest values. This holistic approach integrates the heart's wisdom with the mind's logic, creating a synergy that enhances our ability to achieve greatness. It invites us to consider the broader impact of our choices, not just on our immediate goals but on the world at large.

Creating for the sake of beauty and truth also means embracing innocence and love in our work. It's about approaching our tasks with a sense of wonder and a genuine desire to contribute something meaningful. This mindset shifts our focus from purely strategic outcomes to the joy and fulfillment that come from making a positive difference.

Knowing that beyond rational decision making there is creating for the sake of beauty and truth brings a sense of purpose and fulfillment to our work. It elevates our efforts, infusing them with love and meaning. This path leads to not only personal and professional success but also a legacy of positive impact that endures.

Study me as much as you like,

you will not know me, for I differ in

a hundred ways from what you see me to be.

Put yourself behind my eyes and see me as

I see myself, for I have chosen to dwell in

a place you cannot see.

In the pursuit of creating products and services that resonate deeply with our users, we often embark on a journey of research and analysis, believing that through study, we can fully understand their desires, needs, and experiences. However, this path, while necessary, is fraught with the illusion that we, as creators, can ever completely inhabit the worlds of those we serve. The truth lies in acknowledging that each user's perspective is a complex reality woven from individual experiences, emotions, and contexts – a story that is ever-changing and uniquely personal.

Leading from love, we begin to appreciate that true understanding requires us to look beyond data and demographics. It calls for an empathetic approach, where we strive not just to observe but to connect, to listen not only with the intent to respond but with the openness to be transformed by what we hear. This journey is not about projecting our own assumptions onto the users but about creating spaces where their voices can emerge authentically, guiding us towards solutions that might never have been conceived from our vantage point alone.

Embracing this reality transforms the way we approach design and innovation. It compels us to recognize that our role is not to dictate but to facilitate, not to impose but to discover. It's a shift from seeing ourselves as architects of user experience to becoming gardeners, tending to an ecosystem rich with diversity, nurturing it to flourish in its own unique way. This approach fosters a culture of humility and continuous learning, where every feedback loop is a door to deeper understanding and every iteration is a step closer to meeting our users where they truly are.

This path illuminates the inherent beauty in diversity, underscoring the fact that each user's journey is distinct and valuable. It challenges us to craft experiences that are not only accessible but also inclusive, respecting and celebrating the myriad ways people interact with our creations. By doing so, we not only build products that are loved but also cultivate communities that feel seen, heard, and valued.

The journey towards understanding our users is an ongoing dialogue, a dance of give-and-take that evolves as we grow in empathy and insight. It's a process that reminds us of our own limitations and the boundless possibilities that emerge when we dare to view the world through someone else's eyes. By acknowledging that we are not the user, we open ourselves to a deeper wisdom, one that recognizes the profound connection between serving with empathy and creating with love. This is the heart of innovation – a place of humility, curiosity, and boundless potential, where we learn to see not just with our eyes but with our souls.

Moonlight floods the whole sky

from horizon to horizon;

How much it can fill your room

depends on its windows.

In the vast expanse of the business landscape, opportunities, like moonlight, flood the horizon, illuminating paths previously unseen. The extent to which these opportunities can enlighten and transform our businesses, however, is largely dependent on our willingness to open the windows of perception and venture beyond the familiar confines of our existing operations. This metaphorical gesture of opening windows encourages us not merely to observe but to actively seek and embrace the myriad possibilities that lie in collaboration, innovation, and customer engagement.

Leading from love, we approach the task of seeking new opportunities with a sense of curiosity, empathy, and a genuine desire to create value. This approach is not about opportunistic gain but about fostering meaningful connections and collaborations that resonate with the core values and mission of our business. It's an invitation to explore the landscape with open eyes and an open heart, recognizing that every interaction, every partnership, and every customer feedback is a potential avenue for growth and learning.

This expansive outlook is underpinned by a balanced integration of strategic thinking and spiritual alignment, guiding us to opportunities that not only promise commercial success but also contribute to the greater good. It encourages a leadership style that is agile, responsive, and deeply attuned to the shifting dynamics of the market, enabling us to navigate the complexities of the business world with grace and resilience.

The journey of exploring new horizons demands a culture of appreciation within our organizations, where innovative ideas are nurtured, and the fear of failure is replaced with the courage to experiment. It's a paradigm that values diversity of thought, encourages cross-disciplinary collaboration, and views the business not as a static entity but as a vibrant ecosystem continually evolving in response to its environment.

The act of looking outside our business for new opportunities is a dynamic process of exploration, connection, and transformation. It's a reminder that the potential to enrich and expand our operations is boundless, much like the moonlight that fills the sky from horizon to horizon. The degree to which we can harness this potential is directly related to our willingness to open the windows of our business to the world, inviting in the light of new possibilities and allowing it to illuminate the path to innovation, growth, and lasting success.

I was dead, then alive.

weeping, then laughing.

The power of love came into me,

and I became fierce like a lion,

then tender like the evening star.

Navigating the lifecycle of a business is akin to traversing a vast landscape filled with varying horizons; each presents its own blend of calm and stress, joy and sorrow, success and setback. This journey, marked by such profound contrasts, mirrors the essence of life itself – a marvelous mosaic with pieces of myriad experiences, each color contributing to the beauty of the whole. Within this dynamic ebb and flow, it's the power of love for one's venture that breathes life into the seemingly insurmountable challenges, transforming them into opportunities for growth and innovation.

Leading from love, we approach each phase of the business cycle not just as a series of strategic moves but as a journey of passion and purpose. It's a perspective that allows us to embrace the full spectrum of experiences with open hearts and minds, finding beauty in the moments of triumph as well as in the trials. This approach does not diminish the realities of the hardships faced but offers a lens through which every challenge is seen as a step towards greater understanding and resilience.

The lifecycle of a business, with its highs and lows, demands a balance of fierceness and tenderness – qualities that are seemingly at odds yet are intrinsically connected through the power of love. It is this love that fuels our drive to overcome obstacles with the courage of a lion, and it is the same love that softens our approach, enabling us to lead with empathy and compassion. This duality is not a contradiction but a harmonious blend that enriches our leadership and the culture of our organizations.

The journey through calm and stress teaches us valuable lessons of leading from love, reminding us that true strength lies in our ability to remain balanced and focused amidst the whirlwind of business activities. It encourages us to foster environments where deep respect is paramount, where every team member feels valued and supported through all phases of the business lifecycle.

The myriad horizons of calm and stress that punctuate the lifecycle of a business are not just hurdles to be overcome but are, indeed, the very essence of its beauty. They are opportunities to lead with love, to learn, to grow, and to ultimately create something that transcends the sum of its parts. As we navigate this journey, we are reminded that it is our passion, our resilience, and our capacity for empathy that truly define our success, making every horizon, no matter how daunting, a beautiful part of our collective journey.

Let the lover be disgraceful, crazy, absentminded.

Someone sober will worry about things going badly.

Let the lover be.

In the dynamic world of creation and achievement, there exists a powerful lesson in embracing the essence of what it means to be a lover of one's aspirations, unburdened by the shackles of perfection in process. This passionate approach, seemingly reckless and unfettered, often leads to the heart of innovation, bypassing the well-trodden paths of caution that may lead to mediocrity. It is in this spirit of unapologetic zeal that we find the freedom to explore, to make mistakes, and ultimately, to discover pathways to success that a more cautious approach might never reveal.

Leading from love, we are called to focus on the vision that drives our actions, the outcome that lights up our imagination, and to pursue it with a heart full of passion and a mind liberated from the fear of imperfection. This does not mean we forsake diligence or responsibility, but rather that we allow our love for what we do to guide us through the uncertainties and challenges, trusting that our devotion to our goals will navigate us through the tumultuous waters of innovation and change.

In this approach, the traditional metrics of success and the rigid structures of process give way to a more fluid, organic method of progress, where intuition, creativity, and personal understanding play pivotal roles. It is a methodology that celebrates the journey as much as the destination, recognizing that the most profound achievements are often those that were least expected, born out of a willingness to be led by love and passion rather than by fear and control.

This ethos nurtures an environment where individuals feel empowered to bring their whole selves to their work, to take risks, and to embrace their unique ways of contributing to the collective vision. It fosters a culture of deep care, where the fear of judgment is replaced with the courage to be innovative and the vulnerability to be genuine.

The essence of this approach aligns beautifully with the principles of agility and adaptability, where the focus is on responding to change with grace and flexibility, guided by a clear understanding of the desired outcome. It's a reminder that in the world of business, as in all areas of life, the path to success is not always linear or predictable, but it is always enriched by love, passion, and the courage to let the lover in us lead the way.

The call to let the lover be is a call to embrace our desires and our dreams with open hearts and open minds, to worry less about the perfection of the process and more about the authenticity and intensity of our pursuit. It is in this space of fearless love and passionate engagement that true innovation and lasting success are found.

Advice doesn't help lovers!

They're not the kind of mountain stream

you can build a dam across.

In the vibrant world of innovation and creation, there lies a type of individual whose passion and vision are as unstoppable as a mountain stream. These individuals, fueled by a clear strategy and a heart full of love for their work, embody the essence of what it means to be truly passionate creators. Attempting to alter their course or dissuade them from their chosen path is often an exercise in futility, for their conviction runs deep, and their commitment to their vision is unwavering.

Leading from love, these passionate individuals approach their endeavors with a blend of humility, strategic acumen, and an innate ability to inspire those around them. Their journeys are not defined by the pursuit of simplicity for its own sake, but by the clarity of their vision and the purity of their intention. This approach fosters an environment where innovation thrives, where challenges are met with resilience, and where the collective spirit of a team is dedicated towards achieving shared goals.

The strength of these creators lies in their ability to maintain balance – balancing the head and the heart, balancing strategic planning with the flexibility to adapt, and balancing the pursuit of individual goals with the well-being of the team and community around them. It's a holistic approach that integrates the best of logos, ethos, and pathos, ensuring that every decision is made not just with the mind but with the heart as well.

The passion of these individuals serves as a beacon, attracting like-minded collaborators and customers who are drawn to the authenticity and energy of their work. This magnetic quality opens doors to new opportunities, fosters deep connections, and creates a ripple effect that extends far beyond the immediate scope of their projects. It's a testament to the power of attraction, where positive energy and genuine enthusiasm draw in the resources, people, and circumstances necessary to bring a vision to life.

The passionate creators among us remind us that true innovation and progress often come from a place of deep conviction and love for one's work. They exemplify the idea that when someone is fully aligned with their purpose and strategy, attempting to divert their course is as impossible as damming a mountain stream. Instead, we are invited to learn from their example, to find our own streams of passion and purpose, and to embark on our journeys with a heart full of love, a mind full of clarity, and a spirit ready to embrace the infinite possibilities that lie ahead.

Lovers don't finally meet somewhere.
They're in each other all along.

In the pursuit of innovation, there exists a profound connection between a product and its customer, a kind of predestined harmony where every aspect of the product seems tailor-made for its user. This connection is not the result of chance but the culmination of insight, empathy, and a deep understanding of the customer's needs and desires. It's as if the potential for this perfect match has always been latent, woven into the very fabric of the product and the customer's life, waiting for the moment of discovery to reveal its full significance.

Leading from love, businesses embark on a journey not just to create products but to forge relationships, to understand their customers so deeply that the solutions they offer feel like a natural extension of the customer's own thoughts and desires. This process is grounded in the belief that the essence of a product's value lies not in its features or capabilities alone but in its ability to resonate with the customer, to fulfill a need that perhaps they couldn't articulate but deeply felt.

This level of understanding and connection requires more than market research; it demands an empathetic approach to design and development, one that views customers as partners in a shared journey rather than endpoints in a transaction. It's about creating spaces for dialogue and feedback, where customers feel heard and valued, and where their insights and experiences shape the evolution of the product.

This approach aligns with the concept of care and creativity within organizations, fostering an environment where team members feel empowered to explore, innovate, and express their ideas without fear of failure or judgment. It's a culture that celebrates curiosity and creativity, recognizing that the path to discovering that perfect product-customer fit is often paved with experiments, iterations, and learning from missteps.

The connection between a product and its customer is a reflection of a deeper truth: that the most successful products are those that are developed not just with skill and intelligence but with love and empathy. They are the result of a process that honors the customer's needs, dreams, and aspirations, acknowledging that the potential for a perfect fit has always been present, waiting to be uncovered. It's a reminder that at the heart of every great product is a love story, a story of understanding, connection, and the joy of finding exactly what you've been searching for, as if it's been a part of you all along.

Love comes with a knife, not some shy question,

and not with fears for its reputation!

In the intricate dance of leadership and decision-making, we are often met with questions that do not have easy answers. These wicked questions, complex and multifaceted, challenge us to cut through the surface to the heart of what truly matters. It is here, in the grip of tough decisions, that the essence of our leadership is revealed. Love, in this context, emerges not as a gentle whisper but as a decisive force, a knife that cuts through indecision and fear, guiding us with clarity and conviction.

Leading from love, we find that our moral compass becomes both our shield and our guide. It empowers us to confront challenges not with timidity or concern for our own reputation, but with the courage to do what is right and just. This approach does not simplify the complexity of the decisions we face; rather, it illuminates the path of integrity, enabling us to navigate the labyrinth of leadership with a clear vision and a steadfast heart.

This path, marked by deliberate decision-making informed by a foundation of love, calls upon us to harness our inner strength, to engage with our deepest values, and to lead with a sense of purpose that transcends personal gain. It is a leadership style that embraces vulnerability as a strength, recognizing that the most impactful decisions are those made in the service of others, those that encourage growth and build communities of trust and mutual respect.

This approach to leadership resonates with the principles of self-managed teams, which prioritize human-centric values, collaboration, and the continuous pursuit of improvement. It challenges us to rethink the nature of authority and influence, advocating for a model where power is distributed, where every voice is heard, and where the collective wisdom of the group is leveraged to navigate the complexities of the business landscape.

When love guides our decision-making, we step into a style of leadership that is bold, compassionate, and unafraid to confront the most daunting challenges. It is a leadership that cuts through ambiguity not with force, but with the sharpness of our convictions and the depth of our compassion. It reminds us that at the heart of every decision, every action, and every interaction lies the opportunity to affirm our commitment to the values that define us, to lead not for the sake of personal accolade, but for the profound and lasting impact we can have on the world around us.

In this way, love becomes not just an abstract ideal, but a practical, driving force for good, propelling us and our organizations toward a future marked by integrity, purpose, and transformative change.

Love sometimes wants to do us a great favor:

hold us upside down and shake all the nonsense out.

In the journey of leadership, there comes a moment – a pivotal shift – when we are called to confront the essence of our motivations and intentions. It is a profound process, often sparked by the forces of love, that challenges us to examine the core from which our actions and decisions emanate. This introspective voyage can feel as if we are being held upside down, our perspectives radically altered, compelling us to let go of the clutter of ego, scarcity, and fear that may have quietly taken residence within us. It is in these moments of vulnerability and openness that we are gifted the opportunity to cleanse our vision and realign with our true purpose.

Leading from love, we harness the power of our intuition as a guiding light, a beacon that signals when we stray from our path, ensnared by the trappings of ego or shadowed by fear. This intuitive sense acts not as a critic but as a compassionate mentor, urging us to return to the essence of who we are and what we wish to achieve. It invites us to listen deeply, not just to the words being said but to the unspoken messages of our heart and soul, encouraging us to lead not from a place of scarcity but from abundance and authenticity.

In this space, the foundations of emotional awareness become our tools for navigation, enabling us to discern the subtle differences between decisions fueled by love and those marred by fear. It is a practice that cultivates not only self-awareness but also empathy towards ourselves and others, recognizing that the journey of leadership is as much about inner growth as it is about outward success. This empathetic approach builds a foundation of mutual reliance within our teams and organizations, creating environments where vulnerability is not a liability but a strength, where every member feels seen, heard, and valued.

This process of being shaken free from our 'nonsense' opens the door to a more holistic understanding of success. It challenges us to redefine achievement, not in terms of material gain or status but as the impact we have on the lives of those we lead and serve. It teaches us that true leadership is about cultivating relationships, fostering growth, and creating spaces where individuals can thrive, both personally and professionally.

When we allow love to guide us, to shake loose the constraints of ego and fear, we unlock a deeper, more resonant form of leadership. We become leaders who not only achieve but inspire, not only direct but empower. It is a journey back to our authentic selves, a call to lead from a place of love, integrity, and compassion, creating legacies that are not just remembered for what was accomplished but for how they made others feel, how they lifted others higher, and how they contributed to a world grounded in love and connection.

In the house of lovers, the music never stops,

the walls are made of songs and the floor dances.

In the dynamic world of business, there exists a phenomenon as compelling as it is transformative: when an organization becomes a magnet for individuals whose spirits resonate on the same frequency, the workplace transcends its physical boundaries to become a vibrant ecosystem, alive with energy, creativity, and purpose. This is not the result of mere chance, but the outcome of a culture that values alignment of values, passions, and visions. In such a space, the essence of every task, interaction, and innovation pulsates with the collective heartbeat of its people, creating an environment where the metaphorical music of passion and purpose never ceases.

Leading from love, the foundation of this extraordinary workplace is laid. Here, leadership is not a title or a position but an action that permeates every level of the organization. It's an ethos that champions the beauty of diversity, the strength of empathy, and the power of unity. In this house of collective endeavor, the walls indeed sing with the stories of individual and shared journeys, resonating with the melodies of hard-won successes, lessons learned from failures, and the harmonious blend of diverse talents working towards a common goal.

This environment thrives on the principles of leading from love, where every member feels empowered to express their ideas, share their doubts, and contribute their unique perspectives without fear of judgment or repercussion. It's a place where love and respect guides interactions, ensuring that communication is not just about exchanging information but about connecting on a human level. In such a setting, the floor indeed dances, animated by the dynamic exchange of creativity, innovation, and mutual support.

The alignment with such like-spirited individuals and the cultivation of a vibrant culture is not serendipitous but the result of intentional attraction and selection. It's a testament to the power of clarity in purpose and values, attracting those who are not just looking for a job but for a community and a cause that speaks to their deepest aspirations and values. This synergy amplifies the potential for impact, turning the workplace into a spark for transformation, not just within the confines of the organization but extending out into the world it seeks to serve.

When a business becomes a gathering place for like-spirited people, it transforms into more than just a place of work; it becomes a living, breathing entity, infused with an energy that fuels not just productivity and innovation but also fulfillment and growth. It is a reminder that at the heart of every successful venture lies the spirit of its people, dancing to the rhythm of shared dreams and aspirations, in a house where the music of love and passion never stops.

Those beautiful words we said to one another are hidden in the secret heart of heaven.

One day, like the rain, they will pour our love story all over the world.

In the dynamics of innovation and entrepreneurship, visionaries often find themselves ahead of their time, crafting concepts and solutions that resonate deeply with their own understanding of what the future holds. These ideas, imbued with passion and foresight, may not always find immediate traction or understanding in the present market landscape. Yet, like the most profound expressions of love and connection that find sanctuary in the secret heart of the universe, these concepts await their moment to emerge and transform the world.

Leading from love, innovators are called to embrace the inherent beauty and perfection in their visions, even when the market appears unready or indifferent. This stance is not born of naivety but of a deep-seated belief in the transformative power of their ideas. It's an understanding that the true value of innovation often lies beyond immediate validation, nestled within the potential to catalyze change and inspire new ways of thinking and interacting with the world.

The journey of bringing a groundbreaking business concept to fruition is akin to nurturing a seed beneath the soil. It requires patience, resilience, and an unwavering commitment to the vision, supported by a foundation of human appreciation, strategic insight, and a culture of personal growth that encourages exploration and boldness. This environment allows ideas to germinate, evolve, and, when the time is right, burst forth into the market with the force of a long-awaited rain, nourishing the landscape and reshaping it in ways previously unimagined.

The evolution of such concepts underscores the importance of adaptive strategies – such as agile methodologies and holistic approaches to team dynamics – that enable organizations to pivot, learn, and grow as they navigate the path toward market readiness. It emphasizes the significance of building connections, both within teams and with potential customers and partners, founded on authentic communication and shared aspirations.

The story of an idea too early for its time is not one of failure but of future potential. It is a narrative that champions the beauty of innovation, the courage of creators, and the inevitable unfolding of progress as society grows to embrace new paradigms. The secret heart of heaven holds many such stories, each a testament to the enduring power of love, vision, and the indomitable human spirit to forge new realities. And like the rain that eventually brings life to the dormant seed, the moment will come when these ideas pour forth, painting our collective future with the vibrant hues of change and possibility.

If destiny comes to help you,

love will come to meet you.

A life without love isn't a life.

Leading from love involves trusting that the universe conspires in your favor, even when the path is not clear. It's about allowing love to be the guiding force in your decisions and interactions. This approach fosters an environment where positivity and creativity can flourish, paving the way for a future rich with possibilities.

Simplicity is the key idea that underpins this philosophy. By focusing on the essential aspects of life and business, we can remove the clutter that distracts us from our true purpose. Simplicity brings clarity and direction, helping us to navigate through challenges with ease and grace. It allows us to concentrate on what truly matters – creating value, fostering relationships, and nurturing a culture of love and inspiration.

In the workplace, this mindset transforms how we approach our goals and interactions. When we lead from love and embrace simplicity, we create a culture that values emotional intelligence and psychological safety. This environment encourages team members to express themselves authentically, knowing they are supported and valued. It cultivates a sense of belonging and purpose, where everyone is inspired to contribute their best.

Balancing emotional, intellectual, and spiritual elements in our leadership approach enriches our ability to connect deeply with others and inspire them. Emotionally, it means being attuned to the feelings and needs of those around us. Intellectually, it involves making thoughtful and informed decisions that align with our core values. Spiritually, it's about trusting the process and believing that love will guide us to the right outcomes.

This holistic approach to leadership not only enhances individual well-being but also drives organizational success. When love and simplicity are at the heart of our actions, we attract opportunities and resources that align with our vision. Our teams become more resilient, adaptable, and innovative, capable of turning challenges into opportunities for growth and development.

Engaging with the idea that everything works out in mysterious ways allows us to let go of unnecessary stress and focus on what we can control – our attitudes, actions, and intentions. It encourages us to remain open to new possibilities and to trust that love and inspiration will meet us at every turn. This mindset fosters a positive and proactive approach to both personal and professional life.

Believing in the power of love and simplicity to shape our future leads to a more fulfilling and successful journey. It transforms our work and lives, creating a ripple effect of positivity and inspiration that extends far beyond our immediate environment. This path, guided by love and a belief in the mysterious ways of the universe, promises a future filled with endless possibilities and profound fulfillment.

I once had a thousand desires.

But in my one desire to know you all else melted away.

In the vast expanse of the business landscape, where ambitions run as diverse and deep as the ocean, the clarity of purpose acts as a lighthouse, guiding ships through turbulent seas towards a horizon of fulfillment and impact. This clarity, born from a singular desire to make a difference, to know and serve the core essence of our mission, becomes the most potent force in the universe. When a business aligns itself with a purpose that transcends profit, when it becomes a vehicle for expressing the collective love and passion of its people, it taps into an unparalleled source of energy and focus.

Leading from love, we begin to understand that the true strength of a purpose-driven organization lies not in its strategies or products but in its heart. It's in the shared commitment to a cause greater than ourselves, a commitment that simplifies decision-making, galvanizes teams, and ignites innovation. This singular focus dissolves distractions, aligning every effort, every project, and every person with the core mission. It creates a culture where the love for what we do and who we serve fuels our resilience and creativity, turning challenges into opportunities for growth and impact.

Imagine a business environment so invigorated by its purpose that every task, no matter how small, is imbued with significance. In this space, the complexities of daily operations are navigated with the simplicity of knowing that each step taken is a step towards realizing a shared dream. This is a place where the innocence of our intentions purifies our actions, where the harmony between our emotional, intellectual, and spiritual energies fosters an unstoppable momentum towards our goals.

Such an organization does not merely exist; it thrives, powered by the collective passion of its people, drawing like-minded individuals and opportunities towards it as effortlessly as a flower attracts bees. This magnetic pull is not a matter of chance but a natural outcome of the purity of its purpose, a testament to the principle that when we focus on giving value and operating from a place of love, success becomes a byproduct, not the goal.

This shift in perspective transforms the very nature of work, making it not just a means to an end but an expression of our deepest desires and values. It turns the workplace into a community of like-minded souls, united by a vision that goes beyond the confines of the business itself, touching the lives of people and reshaping the world in its image. In this light, the purpose-driven business stands as a beacon of what is possible when love, passion, and focus converge, offering a powerful reminder that in the pursuit of knowing and serving our true mission, all else indeed melts away.

Be suspicious of what you want.

Leading from love means embracing the present while remaining flexible about the future. When we become overly attached to specific outcomes, we lose touch with the now, and the present is where true power resides. The future, with all its mysteries and uncertainties, can never be fully known. Yet, by crafting strategies and plans that offer direction but remain adaptable, we allow ourselves to respond gracefully to whatever changes come our way.

In business, this means creating frameworks that are both robust and flexible. Plans should be like sails on a ship, catching the wind and propelling us forward, but also capable of being adjusted when the wind changes. A rigid plan may seem secure, but it can quickly become a trap, binding us to outdated ideas and preventing us from seizing new opportunities. Flexibility, on the other hand, enables innovation and resilience.

When we focus too much on the future, we risk neglecting the richness of the present moment. We become fixated on what we think we need, often at the expense of what we already have.

This mindset can lead to a sense of constant striving and dissatisfaction. By grounding ourselves in the present, we find clarity and peace, which in turn allows us to make wiser decisions that align with our true values and long-term vision.

Business strategies that are rooted in the present but open to future possibilities create a dynamic balance. This approach fosters a culture of agility and responsiveness, where teams are empowered to pivot and adapt as new information and circumstances arise. It encourages a mindset of continuous learning and growth, rather than rigid adherence to a fixed path.

Such strategies also nurture creativity and innovation. When teams are not confined by rigid plans, they have the freedom to explore new ideas and solutions. This can lead to breakthroughs that would have been impossible under a more constrained approach. It also builds resilience, as teams learn to navigate uncertainty and embrace change as a natural part of the business landscape.

Moreover, leading from love means valuing the journey as much as the destination. It's about appreciating the process of growth and discovery, rather than being solely focused on specific outcomes. This perspective helps us stay connected to our core purpose and values, ensuring that our actions are not just effective, but also meaningful.

While it is essential to have a vision and direction, it is equally important to remain flexible and present. By crafting strategies that allow for adaptability, we create a business environment that is resilient, innovative, and aligned with our deepest values. Embracing this approach, we can navigate the uncertainties of the future with grace and confidence, knowing that we are always equipped to respond to whatever comes our way.

You think because you understand 'one' you must

also understand two because 1 and 1 equals 2.

But you must also understand 'and.'

In the intricate dance of mergers and acquisitions, the allure of numerical synergy often overshadows the subtler, yet profound, dynamics of integration. It's easy to be captivated by the arithmetic of combining resources, market shares, and capabilities, envisaging a straightforward path to amplified success. However, the true artistry and challenge lie not in the mere aggregation of assets but in the delicate process of interconnecting the distinct cultures, visions, and values of two entities into a coherent, vibrant new creation. This alchemy of unification demands a deep appreciation for the 'and' – the space between the 'one' and 'one' where the potential for a uniquely new creation resides.

Leading from love, we embark on this journey of integration with a recognition that the heart of any organization is its people and their shared sense of purpose. The endeavor of merging two companies thus becomes an exercise in empathy, understanding, and respect. It's about nurturing a shared vision that honors the legacy and strengths of each entity while steering them towards a unified future. This process challenges us to look beyond the balance sheets and strategic alignments, to the very soul of the organizations we seek to blend.

Imagine an environment where this philosophy guides every decision and action in the merger process. Here, simplicity in communication fosters clarity and trust, laying a strong foundation for the integration. The innocence of approaching each new challenge with an open heart and mind paves the way for genuine connections and collaborations. This setting encourages a balance between the emotional, intellectual, and spiritual dimensions of organizational change, ensuring that the merger is not just a transaction but a transformation.

In such a culture, leading from love becomes the critical enablers of success. These values ensure that the organization remains responsive to the needs and concerns of its people, fostering an environment where innovation thrives, and risks are navigated with wisdom and foresight. The design of this new entity, informed by the best practices and unique strengths of both companies, becomes a living example of the leading from love in action, drawing to itself talent, opportunities, and successes that resonate with its elevated aspirations.

By embracing the 'and' in mergers and acquisitions, we unlock the potential to create something greater than the sum of its parts. It's a journey that demands courage, vision, and a profound commitment to the collective future of the newly formed entity. This path, though fraught with challenges, is rich with the promise of creating a legacy that is not only economically successful but also deeply resonant with the values and aspirations of all those it touches.

All people on the planet are children,

except for a very few.

No one is grown up except those

free of desire.

In the hallowed halls of boardrooms, where the future of companies is often decided, there exists a dynamic far more complex than simple decision-making processes or strategic discussions. Beneath the surface of these adult interactions lie the undercurrents of desires and ambitions, driving individuals much like the unseen forces that propel a child in pursuit of a coveted toy. Yet, it is in the rarefied air of those boardrooms, where individuals rise above the fray of personal gain to embrace a broader vision, that true leadership is born. Here, the pursuit is not for financial results alone but for growth, adventure, and the fulfillment of a purpose that transcends the material.

Leading from love, we find the essence of what transforms an ordinary boardroom into an extraordinary one. It's a place where simplicity guides complex decisions, where love for the mission and its people supersedes the love for profits. In such environments, the innocence of exploring uncharted territories is celebrated, fostering a culture where curiosity and learning are the true measures of success. This approach to leadership and decision-making doesn't just aim for short-term gains but seeks to nurture a legacy of innovation, integrity, and impact.

Imagine a boardroom where every member embodies this ethos, where the collective intelligence and empathy of the group pave the way for decisions that are not only financially sound but also spiritually fulfilling. In this sacred space, the balance between the heart and the mind, between intuitive guidance and strategic acumen, is meticulously maintained. Here, the principles of agility and holistic design come into play, ensuring that the organization is not just adaptable and resilient in the face of change, but also aligned with its core values and vision.

Such boardrooms become the breeding grounds for transformative ideas, where the collective pursuit of excellence is driven by a shared passion for adventure and growth rather than by the narrow confines of personal ambition. The energy in these rooms is palpable, charged with the potential to not only change the trajectory of the company but to also leave a lasting impact on the world outside.

In embracing this higher purpose, the leaders within these boardrooms exemplify the profound truth that true maturity and wisdom lie not in the accumulation of desires but in the liberation from them. By fostering a culture that values growth, adventure, and the well-being of all stakeholders over mere financial success, they illuminate a path forward that is both prosperous and meaningful. This is the hallmark of a boardroom not just filled with leaders but with visionaries – individuals who understand that the greatest legacy they can leave is one of positive change and enduring value.

Live life as if everything is rigged in your favor.

Life becomes so easy when you realize that everything is continuously working out for you in mysterious and unexpected ways. This perspective transforms challenges into opportunities and setbacks into opportunities. It instills a sense of trust in the unfolding of events, allowing you to move forward with confidence and grace.

Leading from love means embracing this mindset in all aspects of life, including the business world. It's about fostering an environment where faith in the process and a positive outlook become the foundation for decision-making and strategy. When leaders adopt this approach, they create a culture where team members feel supported and encouraged to explore new possibilities without fear of failure. This belief in the inherent goodness of the journey inspires innovation and resilience.

When you approach your work with the conviction that everything is aligned for your benefit, you naturally exude a sense of calm and assurance. This energy is contagious, influencing your colleagues and creating a harmonious workplace. Challenges are no longer seen as insurmountable obstacles but as puzzles waiting to be solved. This shift in perception can lead to breakthroughs that were previously unimaginable.

In business, this philosophy encourages leaders to trust their intuition and take bold steps towards their goals. It's about recognizing the interconnectedness of all actions and understanding that even the smallest effort can have a significant impact. By maintaining a focus on positive outcomes, leaders can navigate uncertainty with a steady hand, guiding their teams with wisdom and clarity.

Leading from love also involves nurturing a sense of gratitude and appreciation for the present moment. This attitude of gratitude enhances your ability to see the good in every situation, fostering a positive and uplifting atmosphere. It helps you stay grounded and centered, enabling you to make decisions from a place of strength and compassion.

As you move through your professional journey, remember that the universe is conspiring in your favor. Embrace the unknown with an open heart and mind, and trust that each step you take is leading you closer to your ultimate goals. This belief in the benevolence of the universe allows you to remain flexible and adaptable, ready to pivot when necessary and seize opportunities as they arise.

Living life as if everything is rigged in your favor is a powerful approach that can transform your professional and personal life. It encourages you to see the beauty in every moment and to trust in the journey, no matter how unpredictable it may be. By leading from love and embracing this mindset, you create a space where miracles can happen, and where the impossible becomes possible. This perspective not only enriches your life but also inspires those around you to reach their highest potential.

Insights for Leading People & Transformation

Be a lamp, or a lifeboat, or a ladder.

Help someone's soul heal.

Walk out of the house like a shepherd.

These words by Rumi encapsulate the essence of transformative leadership. At its core, the role of a leader is akin to being a source of light, a savior in times of need, or a tool for ascension in the professional world. It's not merely about guiding those we lead to achieve targets and hit quotas. It is about illuminating paths to inner growth, offering support in tumultuous times, and providing the means for individuals to reach new heights in their personal development. The ultimate objective lies in nurturing the workplace as a garden where every individual soul can bloom, where work becomes an expression of one's own journey towards self-actualization.

Leading from love, we step into the workplace not just as managers, but as custodians of our teams' well-being and growth. It's about creating a space where individuals feel seen, heard, and valued. This leadership style isn't about authority. It is about advocacy and empowerment. It's the understanding that each person's contribution is unique and that their personal development is synonymous with the organization's success. It's leading not from the front, not from behind, but from within – standing shoulder-to-shoulder with our teams in the pursuit of a collective vision.

This ethos of leadership is characterized by the gentle touch of a shepherd, who knows when to guide the flock and when to let them find their own footing. It's about fostering an environment that is as nurturing as it is challenging, as forgiving as it is demanding. Such a balance is not found in manuals or metrics but in the subtle art of human connection and the genuine desire to see others succeed.

In this struggle of growth, we are tasked with more than just delegating duties. We are charged with the responsibility to inspire – to ignite the latent potential within each colleague and help them see beyond the horizon of their capabilities. When we do this, we do more than just build a team; we cultivate a community of individuals who are not only adept at their work but are also evolving, becoming more attuned to their strengths and more resilient in the face of their weaknesses.

By embodying the qualities of the lamp, lifeboat, and ladder, we do more than just lead; we transform. We become agents of change in a journey that transcends the confines of office walls, impacting lives in profound and lasting ways. Our work becomes a testament to the power of leadership that is rooted in care, constructed with purpose, and carried out with the passion of a shepherd tending to their flock.

I know you're tired but come, this is the way.

During transformation, the journey often stretches before us, fraught with challenges that test our resolve and push us to the brink of our endurance. It's in these moments, when the weight of progress bears heavily upon our shoulders, that the essence of true leadership emerges – not as a beacon guiding from afar but as a companion walking beside us, sharing in every step of our struggle. This shared journey underscores a profound truth: that real strength lies not in solitary achievement but in collective resilience, in the ability to lift each other up as we navigate the path forward.

Leading from love, the dynamic shifts from merely managing change to nurturing growth through every twist and turn. It's an approach that transcends the traditional paradigms of leadership, recognizing that the heart of transformation lies within the human spirit. This perspective invites a deeper connection, fostering an environment where every voice is heard, every concern is validated, and every individual is seen not just as a part of the process but as a pivotal element of success. It's about creating a space where people feel safe to express their doubts, share their fears, and, most importantly, find the strength to persevere.

Such a culture thrives on the principles of understanding and empathy, where decisions are made not just with the mind but with the heart. It champions the notion that true progress is achieved not by the swiftness of our steps but by the depth of our bonds. This approach doesn't simplify the journey but enriches it, adding layers of meaning and purpose that resonate on a personal level. It ensures that the path, though arduous, is paved with milestones of personal and collective achievements, each one a testament to the power of shared endeavor.

This journey of transformation becomes a canvas upon which the beauty of human potential is vividly painted. It's a process that, while demanding, inspires creativity, encourages innovation, and cultivates a sense of belonging. The challenges encountered along the way become opportunities for learning and growth, shaping a narrative of resilience that weaves through the very fabric of the organization.

Guiding teams through the tumult of change with compassion and empathy illuminates the way forward. It's a path marked by the footprints of those who have dared to lead with their hearts, to believe in the potential of their people, and to embrace the transformative power of collective will. By walking this path together, we not only navigate the present challenges but also lay the groundwork for a future where the full spectrum of human capability is realized, creating not just a successful business but a thriving community of souls united in purpose and passion.

If you have much, give your wealth;

If you have little, give your heart.

In the ever-evolving landscape of business, where the flux of fortune is as unpredictable as the weather, there exists a profound, yet often overlooked principle that can guide companies through both prosperity and scarcity. It's a principle that transcends the tangible metrics of success, urging us to look beyond the balance sheets and into the very heart of what makes a business truly great. This principle champions the idea that the true measure of a company's worth isn't just in its financial assets or market share, but in the wealth of its heart – its capacity to nurture, to give, and to love, irrespective of its phase or wealth.

Leading from love, a concept as radical as it is ancient, invites us to reimagine leadership and compensation not as a transaction, but as a transformation. It beckons us to consider not how much we can accumulate, but how much we can contribute – to our employees, our communities, and the world at large. In the early stages of a company, when resources are scarce and the future uncertain, this might mean offering more than just a paycheck: a share in the vision, a sense of belonging, a commitment to personal and professional growth. It's about creating an environment where trust flourishes, where each member feels seen, heard, and valued, not just for their output but for their intrinsic worth.

As a company grows and prospers, this principle does not diminish; rather, it evolves. It challenges us to leverage our abundance not for unchecked expansion or ostentatious displays of success, but for equitable compensation, for meaningful contributions to society, and for fostering a culture where generosity and kindness are the currencies of value. It's about ensuring that prosperity is shared, that success lifts all boats, and that the heart of the company beats strong and clear in every decision made and action taken.

This approach does more than just create a positive work environment; it attracts like-minded individuals, customers, and partners who are drawn to the company's ethos, setting in motion a virtuous cycle of goodwill and prosperity. It harnesses the collective intelligence, creativity, and passion of its people, catalyzing innovation and resilience in the face of change. It builds companies that endure, not just through economic booms but through the inevitable downturns, because their foundations are built on something stronger than the whims of the market: the unshakeable belief in the power of giving, of contributing to something greater than yourself.

The journey toward true business excellence is one that embraces the simplicity of giving, the strength of love, and the purity of a shared purpose. It's a path that demands courage, for it asks us to lead not from a place of scarcity or fear, but from an abundance of heart. It is here, in the intersection of compassion and commerce, that we find the keys to not just surviving, but thriving in the unpredictable world of business.

when you do things from your soul,

you feel a river moving in you, a joy.

In an age where the pursuit of professional success often leads us down a path of relentless striving and competition, it's easy to lose sight of what truly drives us. We're conditioned to chase after external markers of achievement, to measure our worth by our productivity and our status by our job titles. Yet, deep down, there's a yearning for something more – a longing to engage in work that resonates with our core, work that brings not just financial rewards but profound personal satisfaction and joy.

Leading from love, we begin to see that the real magic happens when we align our professional endeavors with our deepest passions and interests. Imagine a workplace where every individual is encouraged to explore what truly excites them, where the mundane is replaced with the meaningful, and where tasks are not just completed, but are infused with a sense of purpose and delight. It's about breaking free from the conventional chains of job descriptions and roles, and instead, creating an environment where every person is given the liberty to bring their whole selves to their work.

Such a transformation requires us to rethink the very foundations upon which our organizational cultures are built. It means fostering a space where curiosity is nurtured, where innovative thinking is celebrated, and where taking risks is not feared but embraced as a pathway to discovery. It's about recognizing that when people are given the freedom to work on what genuinely interests them, they don't just work – they thrive. They bring an energy and a commitment that can't be mandated or manufactured. Their joy becomes a contagious force, inspiring those around them and elevating the collective spirit of the workplace.

This approach not only enriches the lives of individuals but also propels organizations toward unprecedented levels of creativity and productivity. When people feel connected to their work at a soulful level, they are more engaged, more motivated, and more likely to produce work of extraordinary quality. The ripple effects are profound: higher job satisfaction, lower turnover rates, and a vibrant, dynamic culture that attracts top talent.

Creating space for joy in our work is an act of profound wisdom and compassion. It's an acknowledgment that our greatest contributions come not from the pressure to conform to predefined roles, but from the freedom to explore the vast landscape of our potential. By daring to reimagine the workplace as a place of exploration, creativity, and joy, we not only enhance our own lives but also begin to shape a more vibrant, fulfilling future for all.

The wound is the place where the Light enters you.

In the journey of innovation and growth, the road less traveled is often marked with obstacles and unexpected challenges. These moments, fraught with difficulty and discomfort, are typically viewed with apprehension. Yet, it's precisely within these moments of vulnerability that the greatest opportunities for transformation are found. When faced with adversity, the instinct might be to retreat or to seek a quick fix, but the true path to breakthroughs lies in embracing these challenges, understanding that they are not barriers but gateways to profound innovation and personal growth.

Leading from love, the response to these obstacles transforms the very fabric of how we approach problem-solving and creativity. It's a process that encourages us not only to look for solutions but to understand the deeper lessons these challenges offer. This approach requires a balance, acknowledging the pain points while remaining open to the insights and growth they can catalyze. It's about recognizing that every setback is an invitation to dig deeper into our reservoir of creativity and resilience, to shine a light on the areas that need attention, and to emerge stronger and more enlightened.

This mindset shift is not a solitary journey but a collective endeavor that thrives on collaboration, empathy, and trust. By fostering an environment where vulnerability is seen as a strength and failures as precious gifts, we pave the way for a culture of continuous learning and innovation. It's a culture that values people, understanding that at the heart of every technological advance or business strategy lies the potential for personal and communal growth.

This approach resonates with the understanding that our outer world reflects our inner state. By aligning our actions with our highest intentions and values, we attract opportunities and challenges that propel us forward, not just as individuals but as a collective. It's a recognition that the energy we put into the world, be it through our thoughts, actions, or creations, has a profound impact on what we draw into our lives. Thus, the journey through adversity becomes not just a path to achieving external success but a means of cultivating inner wisdom, resilience, and connection.

The journey of innovation and growth, marked by challenges and setbacks, is not merely a professional endeavor but a deeply personal and spiritual journey. It's a journey that invites us to see beyond the immediate pain or failure, to embrace the light of learning and growth that shines through our wounds. In this way, we come to understand that our greatest challenges are not obstacles but portals, opening us up to new dimensions of creativity, understanding, and connectivity.

christian, Jew, Muslim, shaman, Zoroastrian,

stone, ground, mountain, river, each has a

secret way of being with the mystery,

unique and not to be judged.

In today's global marketplace, the threads of diversity and inclusion weave together to create a fabric that is not only vibrant but also resilient. The rich diversity of backgrounds, beliefs, and perspectives within a team doesn't just add color; it strengthens the very foundation upon which truly great companies are built. Recognizing and embracing this diversity means understanding that each person, regardless of their heritage, culture, or worldview, brings a unique and invaluable contribution to the table. It's about seeing beyond the labels and the surface differences to the profound wealth of experiences and insights each individual offers.

Leading from love, the journey towards embracing diversity and inclusion in the workplace is marked by a commitment to understanding and empathy. It involves creating spaces where everyone feels not just accepted but valued for their authentic selves. This goes beyond mere tolerance or superficial acknowledgments. It is about fostering an environment where every voice is heard, every perspective is considered, and every person is empowered to bring their whole self to work. By doing so, we unlock the potential for innovation, creativity, and problem-solving that is far greater than the sum of its parts.

This approach to building a great company also involves recognizing that the path each person walks is shaped by their experiences, beliefs, and the cultures that have influenced them. It's about appreciating the richness that this diversity brings to our collective endeavors and understanding that our differences are not barriers but bridges to deeper understanding and collaboration. In such an environment, trust flourishes, and with it, the ability to tackle complex challenges with a blend of perspectives that can lead to truly groundbreaking solutions.

Embracing diversity and inclusion is not just a moral imperative but a strategic advantage. It allows companies to better understand and connect with the global mosaic of customers they serve, to innovate in ways that are responsive to a wider array of needs and aspirations, and to stand out in a competitive marketplace as a leader in social responsibility. It's about recognizing that in the diversity of the human experience lies our greatest strength and our most profound opportunity for growth.

Becoming a truly great company in today's world means embracing the full spectrum of diversity and inclusion. It's a commitment to creating a culture where every individual – regardless of their background, belief system, or way of seeing the world – is respected, included, and given the opportunity to shine. This commitment is not just about doing good. It is about being better, stronger, and more connected to the rich smorgasbord of humanity that surrounds us. It's about building companies that reflect the world we want to see: diverse, inclusive, and brimming with potential.

As you start to walk on the way,

the way appears.

In the ever-evolving narrative of business, the process of transformation presents itself as a journey rather than a predefined destination. It's a path laden with uncertainty, where the contours of the future are not etched in stone but are revealed with each step we dare to take. This realization, while daunting, holds within it a profound liberation – the understanding that the act of moving forward, of embracing change, inherently guides us toward the emergence of new pathways, possibilities, and horizons.

Leading from love, we approach this journey of transformation with a sense of openness and curiosity, recognizing that the true essence of growth lies not in meticulously charting every course but in being receptive to the unexpected twists and turns that define our path. It's a leadership ethos that values the journey as much as the outcome, understanding that each step, each decision, and each leap of faith is a vital piece in the story of our organizational narrative.

This perspective encourages a culture of adaptability and resilience, where the focus shifts from attempting to control every variable to cultivating an environment that thrives on flexibility, innovation, and collaborative problem-solving. It's a recognition that the path to transformation is paved with lessons learned, challenges overcome, and the collective creativity and commitment of our teams.

Embracing the unfolding path of transformation aligns with the principles of leading from love, fostering an atmosphere where individuals feel empowered to share their insights, to experiment, and to contribute to the shaping of the journey. It's a paradigm that champions the human basis of business, understanding that at the heart of every strategy, every pivot, and every innovation are people – driven by passion, guided by insight, and united by a shared vision of what could be.

The journey of business transformation mirrors the profound wisdom that as we start to walk on the way, the way appears. It's a call to embrace the inherent uncertainty of change with courage, to lead with love and authenticity, and to trust in the collective ability of our teams to navigate the uncharted waters of innovation and growth. It's a reminder that the path to transformation is not a solitary trek but a shared voyage of discovery, where the true measure of success lies not in the precision of our plans but in the richness of our journey and the depth of our connections along the way.

The beauty you see in me is a reflection of you.

At work and at home, when we appreciate someone for their innate power and beauty, it's a reflection of the same power and beauty within ourselves. This recognition is not just an admiration of others but a profound acknowledgment of our shared potential and worth. It's about seeing the best in others and realizing that these qualities are mirrored in our own souls.

Leading from love means embracing this interconnectedness. It's about understanding that the virtues we admire in our colleagues, friends, and family are also present within us. This awareness fosters a culture of mutual respect and appreciation. When we see the brilliance in others, we are reminded of our own capabilities, which inspires us to strive for greater heights together. This shared journey of growth and appreciation creates an environment where everyone feels valued and motivated.

Simplicity is the key idea that brings this relationship to life. By focusing on the pure, unadulterated essence of what makes us human – our capacity for love, beauty, and potential – we strip away the superficial layers that often cloud our perceptions. Simplicity allows us to connect on a deeper level, seeing each other as we truly are and recognizing the boundless possibilities that lie within.

This perspective transforms how we interact in both personal and professional settings. At work, it encourages us to build teams based on trust and genuine connection. When we appreciate the unique strengths each person brings, we create a dynamic and collaborative environment. This sense of belonging and respect enables innovation and drives success. People are more willing to take risks, share ideas, and support one another when they feel genuinely valued.

At home, this appreciation strengthens our bonds with loved ones. By recognizing and celebrating the beauty and power within our family members, we foster a nurturing and supportive atmosphere. This mutual respect and admiration help us navigate challenges together, reinforcing our connections and deepening our relationships.

Focusing on the innate beauty and power within ourselves and others simplifies our approach to life. It centers us on what truly matters – our shared humanity and potential. This simplicity fosters a sense of peace and clarity, guiding us in our interactions and decisions. It reminds us that we are all connected, and that by lifting each other up, we elevate ourselves.

In every interaction, we have the opportunity to reflect the beauty we see in others. By leading with love and embracing simplicity, we create a world where everyone feels seen, valued, and inspired. This path of mutual appreciation and shared growth transforms not only our workplaces and homes but also our lives, creating a legacy of connection and collective achievement.

Wisdom tells us we are not worthy; love tells us we are.
My life flows between the two.

In the nuanced dance of leadership and management, the challenge often lies in navigating the delicate balance between recognizing the inherent worth of each individual and the pragmatic evaluation of their competencies and contributions. This journey, much like the ebb and flow of life itself, oscillates between the dimensions of wisdom and love, teaching us that true leadership embraces both the understanding of our collective imperfections and the celebration of our boundless potential.

Leading from love, we embark on a quest not just to manage but to genuinely discover and nurture the value and beauty within each person we are privileged to lead. It is a leadership that looks beyond the surface, seeking to understand the unique stories, strengths, and vulnerabilities of our team members. This approach does not shy away from the reality of our human flaws; instead, it views these imperfections as opportunities for growth, learning, and connection.

In this space, the role of a leader transcends the conventional boundaries of management. It becomes a calling to inspire, to empower, and to foster an environment where each individual feels seen, heard, and valued not just for what they do but for who they are. This is where leading from love shines as a light, guiding our interactions and decisions with empathy, compassion, and a deep respect for the dignity of every person.

The cultivation of such an environment demands a commitment to openness and respect, creating a culture where vulnerability is not a weakness but a doorway to authenticity and innovation. It encourages a mindset of continuous improvement, where feedback is shared with kindness and constructive intent, and where failures are not met with judgment but with support and encouragement to try again.

This holistic approach to leadership and management mirrors the dynamic interplay of logos, ethos, and pathos, inviting us to lead with a blend of rationality, ethics, and emotional appeal. It challenges us to see leadership not as a position of power but as a journey of mutual discovery and development, where the goal is not just to achieve targets but to create a legacy of positive impact and human connection.

The art of managing people, when infused with love and guided by wisdom, becomes a transformative practice. It allows us to see the unexplored potential within others, to kindle the flames of their passion and purpose, and to bring together the diverse capabilities of our team into a river of collective success. It is a journey that requires us to navigate the currents between our worthiness and our imperfections, reminding us that in the heart of leadership lies the power to uplift, to heal, and to inspire.

I will soothe you and heal you, I will bring you roses.

I too have been covered with thorns.

On the path of leadership, the journey one embarks upon is not solely for the achievement of goals or the attainment of success; it is, at its core, a profound journey of personal growth and transformation. As leaders, we are uniquely positioned not just to direct and inspire but to nurture and heal, recognizing that the path to growth is often strewn with challenges that can leave individuals feeling vulnerable and exposed. It's a journey that, much like our own, has been punctuated with moments of uncertainty and pain, moments that have imbued us with empathy, resilience, and a deep-seated desire to support those we lead through their thorns to their roses.

Leading from love, we adopt a holistic approach to leadership, one that views each member of our team not just as employees, but as individuals on their own paths of personal and professional development. This perspective invites us to engage with empathy, to listen with compassion, and to act with a genuine commitment to the well-being of our people. It is a leadership style that recognizes the power of vulnerability – both our own and that of those we lead – as a gateway to genuine connection and profound growth.

In creating an environment where leading from love is the bedrock, we cultivate a space where individuals feel free to share their challenges without fear of judgment, where the trials of personal growth are met with understanding and support, and where the journey of overcoming is celebrated as much as the achievements themselves. This approach not only fosters a culture of trust and openness but also empowers individuals to navigate their own journeys of growth with courage and confidence.

This compassionate leadership style is underpinned by the recognition that our own experiences with adversity and growth enrich our ability to guide others. By sharing our stories and the lessons we've learned, we offer not just guidance but also hope, demonstrating that the path through thorns to roses is not only possible but paved with opportunities for learning, healing, and transformation.

The role of a leader transcends the boundaries of traditional leadership. It is a calling to serve as a guardian of potential, a facilitator of growth, and a healer of wounds. By leading with love, empathy, and a deep-seated understanding of the human experience, we not only guide our teams toward their objectives but also support them in their journey toward becoming their best selves. It is in this sacred space of growth and healing that we find the true essence of leadership, where the cultivation of roses from thorns becomes not just a metaphor for personal growth but a lived reality for those we are privileged to lead.

You are my wine, my joy, my garden, my springtime,

my slumber, my repose, without you, I can't cope.

In the heart of every leader lies the power to illuminate the path for others, not merely by the brilliance of their mind but by the warmth of their heart. The true essence of leadership transcends the boundaries of traditional command and control, reaching a place where the bond between a leader and their team is akin to the deep, nurturing connection of a gardener to their garden. It is a place where growth is not just a goal but a journey shared, where the success of each individual contributes to the beauty of the whole.

Leading from love is the art of absolute devotion to your team, fostering a culture where this devotion blossoms into a relentless pursuit of excellence for your customers. Imagine a workplace where every morning feels like springtime, a season of renewal and boundless possibilities. In this space, team members feel like they are part of something larger than themselves, a mission driven by a shared passion and a collective vision of what can be achieved when hearts and minds are aligned.

This approach to leadership asks more of us than traditional methods. It requires a willingness to be vulnerable, to listen deeply and speak truthfully. It means creating an environment where people feel safe to express themselves fully, to experiment and learn from failure without fear of retribution. In such a space, innovation thrives, nurtured by the trust and respect that flows freely among all members of the team.

But how do we cultivate this garden of potential? It begins with the recognition that our people are not just assets to be managed but human beings with dreams, fears, and the desire to make a meaningful contribution. We must strive to understand their needs, to appreciate their unique talents, and to empower them to reach their full potential. This requires a delicate balance, blending the wisdom of experience with the openness to new ideas and ways of working that challenge the status quo.

As leaders, our role is not to be the source of all answers but to be the catalyst for discovery, encouraging our team to explore new horizons and to embrace the journey with joy and enthusiasm. By doing so, we not only achieve remarkable results but also create a legacy of leadership that is rooted in love, respect, and the genuine belief in the unlimited potential of every individual.

The measure of our success is not just in the achievements of our teams but in the depth of the connections we forge along the way. For it is in these connections that we find the true essence of leadership: the ability to inspire, to uplift, and to transform not just our businesses, but the lives of those we are privileged to lead.

Come out of the circle of time and into the circle of love.

In an age where the quantification of work often overshadows the quality of the creative process, there exists a profound shift awaiting those who dare to lead and inspire differently. This transformative shift beckons us to move beyond the confines of time-bound metrics and into the expansive sea of love and growth – a reality where the focus transcends mere presence and productivity, to nurturing the collective creativity and development of individuals.

Leading from love, we embark on a journey of management that prioritizes the growth of people and the richness of what they can create together over the conventional adherence to time recording. It is a philosophy that champions the value of contribution and collaboration, recognizing that the most significant achievements often arise from environments where individuals feel valued, understood, and inspired.

This approach is not merely about eschewing time tracking; it is about fostering a culture where every team member is seen as a whole person, with unique talents, aspirations, and the potential for growth. It is about creating spaces where people are encouraged to bring their full selves to their work, where their contributions are recognized not just for the tasks they complete, but for the ideas they share, the relationships they build, and the impact they have on their colleagues and the broader mission of the organization.

This shift towards managing with a focus on growth and creativity aligns with the principles of leading from love, requiring leaders to cultivate self-awareness, empathy, and social skills. It encourages an environment of creativity, where taking risks, voicing opinions, and experimenting with new ideas are celebrated as essential components of innovation and learning.

Embracing this paradigm opens up new pathways for applying agile methodologies and other forward-thinking management practices that emphasize flexibility, autonomy, and the fluid exchange of roles and responsibilities. It is a testament to the belief that when people are managed with love and a focus on their development, they are more likely to engage deeply with their work, collaborate effectively, and drive the organization towards its vision with passion and purpose.

The invitation to come out of the circle of time and into the circle of love is an invitation to reimagine leadership and management in a way that honors the human spirit. It is a call to recognize that the true essence of work lies not in the hours logged but in the growth experienced, the relationships forged, and the beauty created together. By embracing this perspective, leaders can unlock unparalleled levels of engagement, creativity, and fulfillment, both for themselves and for those they lead, paving the way for a future where work is not just productive, but profoundly meaningful.

Take someone who doesn't keep score,

who's not looking to be richer, or afraid of losing,

who has not the slightest interest even in his

own personality: he's free.

In the swarm of innovation and progress, there lies a breed of individuals whose impact transcends the conventional metrics of success. These are the visionaries and creators who, unfettered by the pursuit of accolades or the fear of failure, dive deep into their passions, propelling themselves and their organizations into new territories of achievement and fulfillment. Their journey is not charted by key performance indicators or benchmarks of wealth but driven by a profound connection to their work that ignites a ceaseless fervor and creativity.

Leading from love, we uncover the essence of what propels these remarkable individuals: a deep-seated passion that serves as both their compass and catalyst. This passion is not a fleeting or superficial enthusiasm but a sustained and purposeful engagement with their endeavors. It's a force that liberates them from the constraints of ego and the anxiety of competition, allowing them to contribute their unique gifts and talents in ways that are both fulfilling to themselves and beneficial to the wider world.

The power of such individuals lies not only in their ability to inspire and innovate but also in their capacity to create environments where others are encouraged to explore and express their own passions. This leadership approach fosters a culture of interconnectedness, where team members feel valued not for their ability to meet predefined targets but for their contributions to a collective vision that resonates with meaning and purpose.

This focus on passion over metrics challenges traditional business paradigms, suggesting that the most significant breakthroughs and advancements come from a place of intrinsic motivation and engagement. It's a model that aligns with the evolving landscape of work, where flexibility, creativity, and emotional satisfaction are increasingly recognized as crucial components of success and well-being.

The journey towards realizing our full potential, both as individuals and as organizations, invites us to reconsider the metrics by which we measure success. It calls us to recognize the immense value of those who approach their work with a heart full of passion, unencumbered by the need for external validation or fear of inadequacy. These individuals remind us that at the core of true achievement lies not the accumulation of wealth or accolades but the freedom to pursue our passions with intensity and integrity. In doing so, they not only achieve greatness in their own right but also light the way for others to follow, creating a legacy of inspiration, innovation, and love that transcends the boundaries of conventional success.

with life as short as a half-taken breath,

don't plant anything but love.

In the labyrinth of leadership, where every turn presents a new challenge and every challenge a potential for growth or setback, the clarity of purpose serves as the guiding light. The most profound decisions, the ones that truly shape the destiny of organizations, are not made in the calm of the boardroom but in the storm of challenges. These are moments that demand more than just analytical prowess; they call for a depth of character and a steadfastness of heart.

Leading from love is about more than just affection or camaraderie. It is about harnessing a force that is as formidable as it is tender, a force that cuts through ambiguity with the precision of a surgeon's scalpel. It's about facing the toughest decisions with a moral compass calibrated to the true north of human values. This compass doesn't waver in the face of adversity; instead, it becomes the beacon that guides teams through the darkest nights.

Imagine navigating the complex world of modern business with this kind of moral clarity. It's about seeing beyond the immediate to the impact decisions will have on people, communities, and the planet. It's about understanding that every choice sends ripples through the ecosystem of our organizations, affecting lives and livelihoods. This level of awareness transforms leadership from a role into a calling, one where the echoes of our actions resonate with the frequency of positive change.

The journey of leadership is as much about cultivating the inner landscape of leaders as it is about influencing the external world. It's about developing the emotional fortitude to face the unknown, the intellectual agility to navigate through complexity, and the spiritual depth to remain centered amidst chaos. This holistic approach empowers leaders to approach problems with a blend of creativity, compassion, and courage.

In a world hungry for genuine leadership, the call to lead from love is both a challenge and an opportunity. It invites leaders to step into their greatness, to lead not just with their minds but with their hearts. It's about creating spaces where people feel valued and heard, where their contributions are not just recognized but celebrated. This environment fosters a culture of innovation and collaboration, where teams are united by a shared vision and driven by a common purpose.

As leaders, we have the opportunity to redefine what success looks like, to build organizations that are not just profitable but purposeful. In doing so, we not only achieve our business objectives but also contribute to a world that is more compassionate, resilient, and sustainable. This is the legacy of leadership that is driven by love – a legacy that, like the sharpest blade, is forged in the fires of our deepest challenges.

Every moment is made glorious by the light of love.

In the intricate dance of life and work, where tasks can often seem monotonous and the days a repeat of the one before, there lies a profound truth waiting to be discovered: every moment, no matter how seemingly mundane, holds within it the potential for joy and fulfillment when illuminated by the light of love. This realization invites us to view our efforts not as obligations to be endured, but as opportunities to infuse every action with purpose and passion. It is a perspective that shifts the focus from the external rewards of our labor to the internal satisfaction derived from performing each task with love.

Leading from love, we discover that the motivation driving our actions profoundly influences our experience of work and life. When our efforts are inspired by love – be it love for the work itself, love for the people we serve, or love for the contribution we make to the world – every task becomes infused with a sense of delight and significance. This approach transcends the binary of liking or disliking certain aspects of our work, inviting us to find depth and meaning in the act of giving our best, regardless of the task at hand.

Embracing this ethos transforms the workplace into a space where the cultivation of self-awareness, the practice of leading from love, and the principles of human-centered design are not just valued, but are integral to the fabric of the organization. In such environments, individuals are encouraged to connect with their work and with each other on a level that goes beyond mere transactional interactions. This fosters a culture of empathy, understanding, and mutual support, where the success of the team is celebrated as a collective achievement.

The principle of acting from a place of love rather than fear has the power to unlock levels of creativity and innovation previously untapped. It encourages a mindset of abundance and possibility, where challenges are approached with optimism and resilience. This shift in perspective not only enhances the quality of our work but also contributes to a more fulfilling and balanced life.

The journey towards finding joy in the mundane lies in our ability to infuse each moment with love. By choosing to approach every task with this intention, we not only enrich our own lives but also inspire those around us to discover the beauty and potential in their own efforts. It is a reminder that the light of love has the power to transform the ordinary into the extraordinary, turning every moment into an opportunity to celebrate the glorious journey of our lives.

Love is the cure, for your pain will keep giving birth

to more pain until your eyes constantly exhale love

as effortlessly as your body yields its scent.

In the pursuit of management and organizational change, the journey toward harmonious and effective transformation often encounters resistance, misunderstanding, and pain. This resistance is not merely a hurdle to be overcome but a signal, an indication of the deep-seated needs and concerns of the individuals within the organization. To address this, a paradigm shift is required – a shift that begins with empathy, understanding, and, most importantly, love.

Leading from love, we recognize that true change within any organization does not start with sweeping decrees or rigid implementations of new processes. Instead, it starts with the hearts and minds of the people it is meant to serve. It begins by meeting them where they are, understanding their daily challenges, and appreciating their contributions. This approach does not see employees as mere cogs in the machine but as vital contributors whose well-being is paramount.

The transformation journey guided by love and understanding acknowledges that for change to be embraced, it must be rooted in the genuine betterment of the work environment and the personal growth of all involved. It seeks to create a culture where feedback is not only encouraged but actively sought, where each voice is heard, and where the fears and anxieties associated with change are addressed with compassion and clarity.

This empathetic approach is bolstered by a foundation of deep self-awareness, which enables leaders to navigate the complexities of human dynamics with sensitivity and insight. It encourages a leadership style that is adaptive, responsive, and grounded in the principles of leading from love, ensuring that all team members feel secure in expressing their thoughts, ideas, and concerns.

The incorporation of methodologies such as Holacracy offer a flexible framework for implementing changes that honor the collective intelligence of the organization. These methodologies advocate for a decentralized approach to decision-making, empowering individuals and teams to contribute to the evolution of their work environment in meaningful and impactful ways.

The path to effective and lasting organizational change is one that is paved with love, empathy, and a deep respect for the individual experiences of each team member. It is a journey that transcends the mere mechanics of change management, reaching into the heart of what it means to lead with purpose and compassion. By adopting this approach, leaders can transform the pain of change into an opportunity for growth, collaboration, and a renewed sense of community within the organization. This is the way forward – a path illuminated by love, where every step taken is a step toward a more inclusive, understanding, and thriving workplace.

I don't want learning, or dignity, or respectability.

I want this music, and this dawn,

and the warmth of your cheek against mine.

In a world that often measures success through the lens of financial gain, fame, and notoriety, there exists a deeper, more resonant form of achievement that transcends the conventional markers of success. This profound realization invites us to reimagine the essence of business, not as a relentless pursuit of material wealth, but as a journey of collective growth and development, where the true riches lie in the connections we forge, the experiences we share, and the lives we touch. It is a vision of enterprise where the melody of genuine human interaction and the dawn of shared aspirations warm the soul, much like the closeness of two individuals sharing a moment of true connection.

Leading from love, we anchor our ventures on the principles of compassion, empathy, and mutual respect, understanding that the heart of any business lies in its people. This approach transforms the workplace into a community where each member is valued not just for their contributions to the bottom line but for their unique presence and potential. It's a space where leadership transcends hierarchical dynamics, becoming a collective endeavor that nurtures growth, fosters innovation, and celebrates each milestone, not as an individual achievement, but as a shared victory.

Embracing this ethos encourages us to cultivate environments that prioritize deep respect, where team members feel empowered to express themselves openly, take risks without fear of judgment, and embrace their vulnerabilities as strengths. It is within these nurturing spaces that creativity flourishes, ideas merge and evolve, and the true potential of a collective vision comes to life. This holistic approach to business, which values personal growth as highly as strategic insight, lays the foundation for an organization that is resilient, adaptive, and deeply connected to its core values.

This paradigm shifts towards valuing human connection and collective growth over traditional markers of success invites a reevaluation of what it means to be truly prosperous. It challenges us to redefine our measures of achievement, to find joy in the journey, and to recognize that the most enduring legacies are those built on the impact we have on others. It's an invitation to create businesses that serve not just as engines of economic growth but as beacons of hope, inspiration, and human solidarity.

The journey toward redefining the essence of business is a call to action, urging us to embrace a vision where success is measured not by the wealth we accumulate but by the depth of our relationships, the strength of our community, and the positive impact we have on the world around us. It's a journey that leads us back to the simple, yet profound, realization that at the heart of every endeavor lies the opportunity to connect, to grow, and to love, transforming not just our businesses, but also ourselves and the world we share.

Love has come to rule and transform;

stay awake, my heart, stay awake.

In all aspects of life and work, change is not just an inevitable force but a dynamic one, propelled by the transformative power of love. This love is not merely an emotion but an active principle that shapes our existence, our interactions, and the world around us. It is through love that we find the strength to embrace change, to grow, and to make meaningful contributions to our communities and beyond.

Leading from love, we acknowledge that every aspect of our lives – including the work we do and the changes we undergo – is infused with the potential for positive transformation. This perspective encourages us to approach our personal and professional challenges with openness, resilience, and a deep-seated belief in the possibility of improvement and innovation.

At the core of this approach lies the integration of simplicity, human awareness, and a holistic view of leadership. By simplifying our goals and processes, we can focus on what truly matters, allowing us to navigate the complexities of change with clarity and purpose. Emotional intelligence empowers us to connect with others on a profound level, fostering environments of mutual respect, understanding, and inclusiveness. Such environments are crucial for encouraging risk-taking, creativity, and collective problem-solving.

Organization designs enabling participative decision-making serve as vital frameworks for managing change in a way that is responsive, inclusive, and effective. These methodologies emphasize the importance of flexibility, rapid iteration, and the empowerment of individuals and teams. They remind us that the essence of adaptability lies in our ability to listen, learn, and pivot in response to new information and changing circumstances.

The journey through change, guided by love, is one of continuous learning and growth. It challenges us to remain awake and aware, to recognize the opportunities for transformation that lie within every challenge, and to commit ourselves to actions that uplift and inspire. It is a journey that calls us to lead with our hearts, to infuse our endeavors with a sense of purpose, and to remember that the most significant changes often begin with small, loving gestures.

In embracing this perspective, we not only navigate the waters of change with grace and confidence but also contribute to a ripple effect of positive transformation. By staying awake to the possibilities of love, we become agents of change, crafting a legacy of growth, beauty, and innovation that transcends our own lives and touches the lives of others. This is the essence of living and working in a world ruled by love.

would you become a pilgrim on the road of love?
The first condition is that you make yourself humble
as dust and ashes.

Would you become a pilgrim on the road of love? The first condition is that you make yourself humble as dust and ashes. Love cannot be from the position of ego or power. Working with people as equals is where to start on the journey of love.

Leading from love means embracing humility and recognizing that true leadership is not about wielding power or authority but about fostering equality and mutual respect. It is about creating a space where everyone feels valued and empowered, where the collective good is prioritized over individual accolades.

Simplicity is the guiding principle that illuminates this path. By focusing on the essence of humility and equality, we strip away the layers of ego and pretense that often cloud our interactions. Simplicity helps us to see each other clearly, as fellow travelers on a shared journey, each with unique contributions and intrinsic worth.

In the workplace, this approach transforms how we lead and collaborate. When leaders humble themselves and engage with their teams as equals, they create a culture of trust and openness. This environment encourages candid communication, innovative thinking, and a sense of shared ownership over the organization's mission and goals.

This approach to leadership fosters deep care and mutual respect within the team. When people feel safe and valued, they are more likely to take risks, share their ideas, and collaborate effectively. This not only enhances individual well-being but also drives organizational success, as the collective creativity and energy of the team are harnessed toward common goals

Engaging with the idea that love cannot come from a position of ego or power also means embracing vulnerability. It requires leaders to acknowledge their limitations and be open to learning from others. This vulnerability fosters deeper connections and a more authentic, supportive work environment.

Working with people as equals creates a ripple effect of positive change. It inspires others to lead with humility and compassion, creating a culture where everyone feels seen, heard, and appreciated. This path, guided by simplicity and love, transforms our work and our lives, making us not only better leaders but also better human beings. The journey of love in leadership is about building a future where respect, collaboration, and shared purpose illuminate the way forward.

when we practice loving kindness and compassion
we are the first ones to profit.

Leading from love means cultivating a workplace where fairness and empathy are not just encouraged but are foundational to every interaction and decision. When leaders embody these virtues, they not only foster a supportive environment but also witness a transformation within themselves. This shift is not just in how they relate to others, but in how they perceive and engage with the world around them.

By prioritizing compassion, leaders ignite a powerful force within themselves and their teams. This force, a deep sense of connection and understanding, paves the way for genuine interactions and a collaborative spirit. It's in this space that the magic of innovation and creativity flourishes. Teams feel more secure to express their ideas, take risks, and commit wholeheartedly to the organization's mission because they know they are valued and understood.

Moreover, this practice of compassionate leadership goes beyond the immediate benefits of improved team dynamics. It touches the very core of the leader's personal growth. As leaders nurture their teams with kindness and fairness, their own inner life becomes enriched. They develop a keener intuition for making decisions that align with both their values and the needs of their organization. This harmonious alignment enhances their ability to foresee and act upon opportunities that might have otherwise been overlooked.

This leadership style also creates a ripple effect throughout the organization. A culture of kindness and respect, once established, becomes self-perpetuating. New leaders emerge from within these compassionate environments, equipped with the emotional maturity to continue this legacy. Thus, a cycle of positive growth sustains itself, underpinned by the principles of love and respect.

The practice of loving kindness and compassion in leadership is an ongoing journey. It requires patience, commitment, and a willingness to be vulnerable. Leaders must continually engage with their teams and with themselves, learning and adapting as they go. This path is not without its challenges, but the personal and professional rewards we reap from this approach are profound.

Embracing the transformative power of compassion in leadership not only fosters a healthier, more vibrant workplace but also cultivates a deeper sense of fulfillment and purpose in leaders. As they grow in their ability to lead with love, they find that their own lives are enriched, embodying the truth that in giving we receive.

I am not this hair, I am not this skin,

I am the soul that lives within.

Leading from love means recognizing that beyond the visible markers of diversity lies the profound truth that every individual within a company is a unique and valuable soul. This realization transforms the way we approach inclusivity, shifting it from a surface-level initiative to a deep, soul-affirming practice. In the hustle of daily business, it's easy to categorize people by their roles, appearances, or backgrounds. However, true inclusivity goes beyond these external factors and honors the intrinsic worth of every team member.

When leaders embrace this deeper understanding, they cultivate an environment where each person's unique essence is acknowledged and valued. This not only enhances individual well-being but also fosters a collective spirit of unity and purpose. In such an environment, people are more likely to bring their whole selves to work, contributing their full range of talents and perspectives.

In this light, diversity is not just a metric to be achieved but a celebration of the rich variety of human experience. Inclusivity becomes an act of love, recognizing the soul within each person and creating space for their full expression. This approach nurtures a culture of genuine connection, where employees feel seen and appreciated for who they truly are, beyond their external attributes.

This profound respect for individuality requires leaders to cultivate deep care and empathy. By tuning into the subtle, non-verbal ways that people express their needs and aspirations, leaders can respond with understanding and support. This deep listening fosters an atmosphere of respect and inclusivity, where team members feel comfortable sharing their ideas and concerns without fear of judgment.

The impact of such an inclusive environment is far-reaching. When people feel valued at their core, their engagement and motivation soar. They are more likely to take risks, innovate, and collaborate effectively, knowing that their contributions are appreciated. This creates a positive feedback loop, where the organization thrives on the collective strength of its diverse and fully engaged members.

As leaders continue to honor the unique souls within their organizations, they pave the way for a more compassionate and inclusive future. This journey is not without its challenges, but the rewards are profound. By fostering an environment where every individual is seen and valued for their inner essence, leaders can create workplaces that not only succeed but also inspire and uplift.

In essence, the true power of diversity and inclusivity lies in the recognition and celebration of the soul within each person. This understanding transforms leadership into an act of love, nurturing the spirit of every individual and the collective whole.

There is little one can say about love.

It has to be lived, and it's always in motion.

In business, just as in life, the only constant is change. The people within our organizations evolve; their dreams grow, their needs shift, and their skills develop. Simultaneously, the market around us is a living entity, pulsing with new demands, trends, and challenges. Embracing this perpetual motion not as a hurdle but as a dance is the essence of a vibrant, thriving business. This continuous adaptation, this endless cycle of growth and transformation, is not just a strategy. It is an act of love. It's a commitment to nurturing an environment where people and ideas flourish, where the journey itself becomes as important as the destination.

Leading from love, we acknowledge that the heart of our business beats strongest when we are in harmony with this ever-changing landscape. It's about recognizing that the deepest connections with our teams and customers are forged not through transactions, but through shared experiences and journeys. It's a leadership that cherishes the human spirit, that listens with empathy and acts with compassion. This approach transforms challenges into opportunities for innovation, and uncertainty into a canvas for creativity.

Imagine creating a space where simplicity guides complexity, where the innocence of our initial visions remains untarnished by cynicism. This is a place where the voices of reason, emotion, and spirit find equal footing, creating a holistic path forward. In such a space, adaptability and resilience are not just buzzwords but lived experiences, reflected in the way we embrace agile methodologies not just in our processes but in our thinking. Here, leadership is not about imposing control but about facilitating growth, where every member of the team is empowered to contribute, to learn, and to lead in their own right.

This dynamic environment is where true innovation flourishes, driven by a collective desire to make a meaningful impact. It's built on the foundation of understanding that our work is never truly done, that there's always a new horizon to explore, a new lesson to learn, and a new way to grow. It's here, in the midst of this continual evolution, that we find the most profound expression of love in business. It's a love for the journey, for the people we share it with, and for the lives we touch along the way.

As we align our actions with this fluid, loving approach to business, we attract success in ways that are profound and lasting. We create not just a legacy of achievements, but a legacy of meaningful connections and transformative experiences. This is the heart of a thriving business, pulsing with the rhythms of change, guided by love, and ever in motion.

Your acts of kindness are iridescent wings of divine love, which linger and continue to uplift others long after your sharing.

In the heart of every thriving organization beats the pulse of its people, a rhythm composed of individual growth, collective purpose, and the myriad acts of kindness that bind them together. The success of a company, its ascent from the roots of ambition to the heights of achievement, is inextricably linked to the growth and well-being of those who dwell within its walls. Each supportive gesture, each moment of encouragement, weaves a fabric of resilience and solidarity that propels the entire organization forward. These acts, seemingly small and often unnoticed, are the beads from which the necklace of a company's legacy is created.

Leading from love, we realize that the foundation of any successful enterprise is not built on the cold calculus of profits and losses but on the warm, irreplaceable currency of human connection. It's in the moments we choose to lift each other up, to extend a hand in times of struggle, and to celebrate together in times of triumph, that we truly define the essence of our organization. This ethos of mutual support and kindness fosters an environment where innovation is nurtured, where challenges are met with collective resolve, and where each individual's potential is recognized and revered.

Imagine a workplace where the norm is to act with generosity of spirit, where the guiding principle is that the success of one contributes to the success of all. In such a place, the barriers between roles and hierarchies blur, replaced by a shared commitment to growth and excellence. Here, the simple acts of listening, sharing knowledge, and offering encouragement become powerful catalysts for transformation, both personal and professional. This is an environment where the balance between achieving ambitious goals and maintaining a nurturing, supportive culture is maintained with grace and ease, guided by leaders who understand that the heart of leadership is service.

In this culture, the ripple effects of kindness are felt far beyond the immediate context of their offering, continuing to uplift and inspire long after the moment has passed. It's a setting leading from love is truly lived, creating a workplace that is not only productive but profoundly human.

By fostering this spirit of kindness and support, we unlock not just the potential of our colleagues but the potential of our organization as a whole. We build a legacy not measured in quarterly earnings but in the lives touched, the careers developed, and the community fostered. This is the true measure of success, a testament to the enduring power of acts of kindness and the divine love that animates them, ensuring that our collective efforts continue to uplift long after our individual contributions have been made.

Those who don't want to change, let them sleep.

In the vibrant landscape of business transformation, where the winds of change blow strong and the horizon teems with untapped opportunities, the journey of reinvention beckons. It's a call to adventure, a summon to cross new thresholds and venture into uncharted territories. This path, however, isn't for everyone. Some may find the call too daunting, the risks too great, or the unknown too unsettling. And that's perfectly okay. The essence of true transformation lies not in converting the reluctant, but in uniting the willing, those ready to embrace change with open arms and embark on a journey of collective evolution.

Leading from love, the journey of transformation becomes not just about achieving new milestones but about how we navigate the path together. It's about creating spaces where curiosity is nurtured, where innovative ideas flourish under the care of those bold enough to dream them. In these spaces, each individual's contribution becomes a vital thread in the fabric of our collective story, woven with strands of mutual respect, understanding, and genuine human connection. This approach fosters a culture where the fear of failure is replaced with the courage to experiment, and where the joy of discovery is shared.

But what of those who choose to stand back, who prefer the comfort of the known to the uncertainty of new beginnings? It's crucial to recognize that their time may come, but now is not it. And in acknowledging this, we free ourselves to move forward with those who share our vision and passion for change. This is not about leaving anyone behind. It is about respecting each person's journey and recognizing that not everyone is ready to take that leap at the same moment.

In celebrating those who join us, we build more than just a team; we build a community. A community that thrives on collaboration, where success is measured not only in achievements but in the strength of our relationships and the depth of our connections. Here, leadership transforms into a shared journey, where guiding is not about dictating the way but about lighting the path so others can find their own way forward.

Thus, as we venture forth, let us cherish those who walk with us, knowing that our combined steps echo the heartbeat of our shared aspirations. Let us create not just a narrative of success but a legacy of inspiration, where the spirit of transformation ignites a flame in others to pursue their own paths of change. In this journey, our collective resilience, creativity, and passion become the landmarks of our progress, guiding us toward a future where the possibilities are as limitless as our willingness to explore them. Together, we embark on this adventure, ready to shape the world with the strength of our vision and the power of our collective spirit.

Everyone has been made for some particular work,

and the desire for that work has been put in every heart.

In the masterpiece of organizational life, the brushes that
paint the most compelling patterns are those aligned with the
intrinsic motivations and unique capabilities of each individual.
The artistry of management, then, lies not in the imposition of
tasks or the dictation of paths but in the delicate act of aligning
the work with the worker, in recognizing and nurturing the
innate passions and strengths that each person brings to the
table. This alignment, a confluence of personal joy and
professional excellence, is where the true magic of management
unfolds, transforming everyday tasks into a symphony of
productivity and fulfillment.

Leading from love, we approach the task of management as a
journey of discovery, a process of unveiling the work that not
only needs doing but that calls to the heart of the individual
tasked with its completion. It's about seeing beyond resumes and
job descriptions to the deeper currents of potential that flow
within each member of our team. This approach transforms the
workplace into a garden where every plant is carefully placed in

the soil where it will thrive the most, where the unique contributions of each individual are recognized, valued, and cultivated.

Imagine a workplace where every assignment starts with the question, "Who will find joy and fulfillment in this task?" In such an environment, the simplicity of matching tasks with natural inclinations leads to a profound increase in efficiency, engagement, and quality of work. Here, the innocence of pursuing one's passions is protected and cherished, seen not as a luxury but as a fundamental ingredient for success. This space is one where the balance between the heart's desires and the mind's capabilities is gracefully maintained, creating an atmosphere where innovation and contentment flourish side by side.

This philosophy of leadership and management transcends traditional paradigms, inviting us to envision a world where work is not a place of drudgery but a playground of opportunity, where every individual is empowered to contribute their best, propelled not by the fear of failure but by the love for what they do. In such a world, the emotional, intellectual, and spiritual dimensions of work are harmoniously aligned, fostering an environment where people do not merely survive but thrive, where the workplace becomes a reflection of the best aspects of human potential and creativity.

By embracing this approach, we unlock a powerful dynamic within our teams and organizations, one where the natural desires and abilities of each individual are the guiding stars of their professional journey. This alignment not only enhances the well-being and satisfaction of each team member but also propels the organization towards its collective goals with an unmatched vigor and passion, proving that the greatest achievements are born from the marriage of individual fulfillment and collective ambition.

Know then the body is merely a garment.

Go seek the wearer, not the cloak.

In the intricate dance of human interaction, especially within the dynamic arenas of our professional lives, it's all too easy to focus on the external – the titles, the attire, the superficial markers of success and authority. Yet, beneath these layers, lies the essence of who we are, the spirit that animates our actions and defines our true worth. Recognizing this essence in others, beyond the external veneer, is a journey of deep connection and understanding, a path that leads to the heart of genuine relationship and collaboration.

Leading from love, this journey transforms the way we interact with the world around us. It shifts our focus from what is seen to what is felt, from the garment to the wearer. In doing so, it challenges us to look beyond first impressions, to seek the underlying truth of each person's character and intentions. This approach does not negate the importance of professionalism or the need for boundaries; rather, it enriches our interactions, making them more meaningful and impactful.

In cultivating environments where this level of connection is encouraged and valued, we not only enhance our personal well-being but also elevate the collective spirit of our workplaces. It becomes a space where creativity flourishes, where innovation is born from a place of trust and mutual respect. Here, challenges are not roadblocks but opportunities for growth, and differences are not divides but bridges to deeper understanding.

Such an approach to business and to life requires a paradigm shift – a move away from judgment and towards empathy, from competition to collaboration. It asks that we see each person not as a role or a function but as a unique individual, with their own stories, dreams, and challenges. By doing so, we unlock the potential for profound connection, for relationships that transcend the transactional and become truly transformational.

This ethos of seeing beyond the surface to the spirit within has far-reaching implications. It influences how we lead, how we follow, and how we interact with each other on every level. It fosters a culture of being a true team, where people feel seen, heard, and valued for who they are, not just for what they can do. This is the foundation of a truly human-centered approach to work, one that celebrates the individual but thrives on the collective.

The pursuit of connecting with the inner spirit of another is not just a noble endeavor. It is a practical strategy for building stronger, more resilient, and more innovative organizations. It's a reminder that in the midst of our busy, often chaotic professional lives, the most powerful connections are those that touch the heart and stir the soul. By seeking the wearer, not the cloak, we discover the true essence of leadership, partnership, and human connection.

Yesterday I was clever, so I wanted to change the world.

Today I am wise, so I am changing myself.

In the ever-evolving landscape of business, where change is the only constant, the most transformative power lies not in the grandeur of our ambitions to change the world but in the humility of our efforts to change ourselves. This inward journey, a quest for personal growth and self-improvement, sets the foundation for the kind of leadership that inspires, motivates, and drives sustainable change. It's a realization that before we can effect lasting change in our organizations and the world at large, we must first cultivate the values, behaviors, and attitudes we wish to see in others within ourselves.

Leading from love, we embark on this transformative journey with the understanding that the essence of impactful leadership is rooted in the authenticity and integrity of our personal development. It's a process that requires us to confront our limitations, to embrace vulnerability, and to continuously strive for a higher version of ourselves. This path of self-evolution not only enhances our capacity to lead with empathy and understanding but also empowers us to create environments where trust, innovation, and collaboration flourish.

Imagine a workplace where each member, from the newest intern to the seasoned executive, is committed to personal growth and self-reflection. In such a space, the simplicity of being true to yourself becomes the cornerstone of complex organizational change. Here, the innocence of admitting what we don't know paves the way for learning and innovation, while the harmony between our personal values and our professional actions fosters a culture of integrity and excellence.

This philosophy of internal transformation as the catalyst for external change challenges us to view our roles not just as job titles but as opportunities to embody the principles we advocate for. It's an invitation to lead by example, to demonstrate through our actions the power of personal accountability, and to inspire those around us to embark on their own journeys of self-discovery and growth.

By embracing this approach, we unlock a profound and often overlooked dimension of leadership, one where the process of changing ourselves becomes the most potent tool for shaping the future of our businesses and the world. It's a testament to the idea that the greatest impact we can have starts with the courage to look inward, to nurture the qualities we aspire to see in others, and to be the change we wish to see in the world. In this way, our personal transformation becomes a beacon of possibility, illuminating the path for others and contributing to a legacy of positive change that transcends the boundaries of our immediate environments.

Insights for Leading Customers & Operations

Since I have learned to love you,

I have closed my eyes to everyone else.

In a world overflowing with choices and distractions, true strength lies in focusing on a single, ideal customer profile. This approach is not about limiting your reach but about deepening your impact. By dedicating your energy to one ideal customer, you create a bond so profound that it becomes the foundation of your business's success.

Leading from love involves a deep commitment to understanding and serving this chosen customer with genuine passion and empathy. It's about seeing them not just as a target market but as a partner on a shared journey. This relationship transcends mere transactions. It involves immersing yourself in their dreams, understanding their challenges, and anticipating their needs. This deep empathy allows you to create products and services that resonate deeply, forging an emotional connection that fosters unwavering loyalty and trust.

Simplicity is the key idea that transforms this relationship. By focusing on one ideal customer, you strip away the unnecessary and superficial, leaving a pure and powerful connection. Simplicity fosters innovation by allowing you to concentrate on what truly matters, pushing boundaries with confidence and clarity. This focused approach concentrates your efforts, creating a more meaningful and impactful connection.

This singular focus brings clarity and direction to your business efforts. Instead of scattering resources, you channel them with precision, driving innovation and excellence. Your business becomes a finely tuned instrument, playing a melody that speaks directly to your customer's heart. Each touchpoint feels personal, and every interaction is infused with genuine care and attention.

Creating a safe space for your customer – a sanctuary where their needs are understood and met with compassion – is fundamental. This space builds lasting relationships through consistent, thoughtful actions. It's about showing your customer they are valued, not just as a source of revenue, but as an essential part of your mission. This nurturing environment fosters trust and a deep sense of belonging.

Focusing on one customer profile accelerates growth rather than limiting it. As you refine your approach with this core group, the insights you gain become the foundation for broader success. Lessons learned from this focused service inform every decision, driving sustainable and meaningful growth. Your business evolves into a dynamic, responsive entity that adapts and thrives.

In a crowded marketplace, the art of focusing on one ideal customer profile sets you apart. It transforms your business into a guiding light, enhancing customer satisfaction and fostering continuous improvement. This dedication to a singular focus cultivates an environment where simplicity and love are paramount, leading to profound and lasting impact.

If you desire healing, let yourself fall ill.

In the fast-paced world of business, where the relentless pursuit of perfection often overshadows the journey towards improvement, there lies a hidden wisdom. This wisdom suggests that true progress is not about avoiding of flaws but about embracing them as opportunities for growth and learning. It's about understanding that to move forward, we sometimes need to allow ourselves to be vulnerable, to acknowledge our imperfections, and use them as stepping stones towards something greater.

Leading from love, we embark on a journey that challenges conventional notions of leadership and success. It's a path that demands courage – the courage to face our shortcomings head-on and the wisdom to know that these very shortcomings can be the source of our strength. This approach is not about lowering standards but about creating a culture where mistakes are not feared but are seen as vital for learning and innovation. It's about building an environment that encourages taking risks and supports individuals through their failures, knowing that each misstep brings us closer to our goals.

Such a mindset requires a delicate balance of human awareness, fostering a space where empathy and understanding are paramount. It encourages us to lead with compassion, recognizing the inherent value in each team member's journey. This approach does not merely enhance the collective spirit but also drives performance, as individuals feel genuinely supported and valued. The result is a team that's not only resilient in the face of challenges but also more agile and innovative, ready to adapt to the ever-changing business landscape.

This philosophy nurtures an organizational culture steeped in respect and acceptance, where team members feel safe to express their ideas, concerns, and vulnerabilities without fear of retribution. In such an environment, creativity and collaboration flourish, paving the way for groundbreaking ideas and solutions. It's a culture that recognizes the importance of the human element in achieving business success, valuing the well-being and personal growth of its members as much as, if not more than, the bottom line.

The journey towards continuous improvement is not a linear path free of obstacles but a winding road filled with challenges and learning opportunities. It's a journey that requires us to embrace our imperfections, to learn from them, and to allow them to propel us forward. By fostering a culture of love, empathy, and safety, we create a space where continuous improvement is not just a goal but a natural outcome of our collective efforts. In doing so, we not only achieve greater business success but also contribute to a more compassionate and understanding world.

I closed my mouth and spoke to you

in a hundred silent ways.

Realizing that people in a business share their needs in non-verbal ways opens a new dimension of understanding and empathy within the workplace. The subtle cues, the unspoken words, and the silent gestures all paint a rich chorus of communication that speaks volumes about the true needs and feelings of individuals.

Leading from love means tuning into these non-verbal signals with a heart full of empathy and a mind open to deeper connections. It's about going beyond the surface-level interactions and truly seeing and valuing the unspoken needs of your colleagues and employees. This form of leadership fosters a culture where everyone feels understood and supported, even without words.

Simplicity is the key idea that brings clarity to this approach. By focusing on the pure and essential aspects of human interaction, we can strip away the noise and distractions that often cloud our perceptions. Simplicity helps us to hone in on what truly matters: the genuine connections and shared understanding that form the foundation of a healthy, productive workplace.

This attentiveness to non-verbal communication enriches the workplace environment. It cultivates respectful intimacy, allowing leaders and team members to respond to the unspoken needs with sensitivity and care. This heightened awareness creates a sense of togetherness, where individuals feel secure and valued, knowing their silent signals are acknowledged and respected.

This means creating a work culture that values and responds to non-verbal communication. Agile methodologies, for example, emphasize the importance of team dynamics and continuous feedback, both verbal and non-verbal. By integrating these practices, organizations can build a responsive and adaptive environment where silent signals are as powerful as spoken words.

This approach transforms the workplace into a space of mutual respect and understanding. It encourages leaders to look beyond the obvious and engage with the deeper currents of human interaction. By acknowledging and addressing the non-verbal needs of their teams, leaders foster a more inclusive and compassionate work environment.

Realizing that people in a business share their needs in non-verbal ways is a call to lead with greater sensitivity and awareness. It invites us to listen with our hearts and minds, to see beyond the spoken words, and to connect with the essence of those we work with. This path, guided by simplicity and love, transforms the workplace into a haven of understanding and growth, where every individual feels seen, heard, and valued.

A thousand half-loves must be forsaken to
take one whole heart home.

In the vast landscape of business, where the horizon is dotted with countless opportunities and the paths of service are many, there emerges a guiding principle that cuts through the complexity with the precision of a well-honed blade. It is the understanding that true excellence in service cannot be spread thinly across the multitude but must be poured generously into the cup of the truly perfect customer. This realization is not the narrowing of vision but the focusing of intent, ensuring that every ounce of effort is channeled where it will shine brightest and resonate most deeply.

Leading from love, the journey towards identifying and serving this ideal customer transcends the mere mechanics of business operations. It becomes a quest of alignment, where the values, desires, and aspirations of the provider and the served become so intertwined that the act of service becomes a reflection of a shared essence. This is not a process dictated by data alone but one that is felt, a resonance that is as much about emotional and spiritual connection as it is about transactional exchange.

This focused approach does not come without its challenges. It requires the courage to move beyond the safety of broad appeal, to embrace the vulnerability of placing all hopes in the connection with a narrower audience. Yet, it is within this space of focused intent that the magic of true connection occurs, where the service provided is not just appreciated but cherished, not just consumed but celebrated.

Such a path demands an adherence to principles that go beyond the traditional metrics of success. It calls for a dedication to understanding and empathy, a commitment to creating experiences that are not just effective but transformative. This is where the heart of innovation beats strongest, where creativity is unleashed not by the desire to appeal to all but by the passion to move one.

The journey towards serving the perfect customer is a testament to the power of purposeful action and the belief that when service is rendered with a full heart, it echoes far beyond the immediate interaction. It becomes a beacon, attracting those who share the vision and values at the heart of the service, creating not just a customer base but a community. This is the way home for businesses seeking not just to succeed but to truly matter, to leave a mark on the hearts of those they serve and to craft a legacy built on the foundation of meaningful connections.

Don't be satisfied with stories,

how things have gone with others.

Unfold your own myth.

In an age where the shelves are laden with guides on achieving success and consultants are ever ready to offer their playbook, it's easy to fall into the trap of living vicariously through the victories and failures of others. The stories we read and the advice we heed often shape our aspirations, yet they also risk confining us to the pathways others have tread. This mimicry, while comforting in its familiarity, seldom leads to the creation of something truly unique or groundbreaking. In essence, by solely relying on external narratives, we risk sidelining the most powerful protagonist in our story: ourselves.

Leading from love, the journey to genuine innovation and growth begins not in the boardroom or the marketplace, but within the quietude of our own minds. It's a journey that asks us to peel back the layers of what we've been taught to seek out what we truly love. This isn't about the pursuit of profit or prestige, but about connecting with our core, where our simplest yet most profound aspirations lie. By fostering this deep connection, we nurture an environment where creativity flourishes, unencumbered by the need to replicate existing models.

The most transformative ideas often emerge from this space of harmony. It is a place where the heart, mind, and spirit converge, offering a clarity that cuts through the noise of the latest trends and methodologies. This clarity allows leaders to craft visions that are not only innovative but deeply resonant with their teams, stakeholders, and communities. Such visions inspire action not because they are directive but because they are magnetic, drawing others into a shared journey of discovery and creation.

This approach to leadership and innovation is akin to navigating by the stars rather than following well-worn trails. It requires a blend of courage and vulnerability, an openness to exploring unknown territories without a map. Yet, it is in this exploration that teams find themselves more agile, able to pivot with the shifting sands of the market while maintaining their coherence and integrity. It fosters a culture where feedback is not just heard but deeply felt, where every member feels seen, understood, and integral to the collective mission.

Embracing this path means viewing every challenge as an opportunity to learn and every failure as a stepping stone to greater understanding. It cultivates a mindset where attracting success is not about employing the right tactics but about aligning with a higher purpose, one that transcends the individual and speaks to the collective aspiration of humanity to create, connect, and thrive. In this light, success is not just measured by the bottom line but by the depth of impact and the breadth of innovation it inspires.

what you seek is seeking you.

In a world saturated with advertisements and marketing strategies all vying for the consumer's attention, the quest for authenticity and connection often gets lost in translation. The pervasive approach to marketing has traditionally been about persuasion, about crafting messages that nudge, cajole, or even trick people into making a purchase. However, this method, focused on short-term gains, overlooks a fundamental human desire for genuine connection and understanding. It's a desire that, when acknowledged and embraced, can transform the very fabric of how we think about engaging with our audience.

Leading from love, the shift towards allowing people to engage with us rather than attempting to manipulate them marks the dawn of a new era in business. This approach is not about diluting your message or abandoning strategies. It is about infusing your interactions with honesty and integrity. It's about recognizing that the foundation of any lasting relationship, be it personal or professional, is mutual respect and understanding. By adopting a mindset that prioritizes these values, companies can create a space where customers feel seen, heard, and valued, not just as consumers but as individuals with their own stories, desires, and needs.

This change in perspective requires a balance between self-awareness and a deep understanding of the human psyche. It asks us to listen more than we speak and to foster environments where people feel safe to express themselves and explore. It's about creating narratives that resonate not because they are perfectly polished but because they are profoundly human. In such a space, the barriers between the company and the consumer begin to blur, leading to relationships that are built on trust and mutual benefit.

This approach acknowledges that the essence of what we offer is already sought after by those who need it most. By focusing on being authentic and transparent in our intentions and actions, we attract those who are in alignment with our values and vision. This is not a passive strategy but a dynamic engagement that recognizes the active role of attraction in shaping our business landscape. It's a recognition that the energy we put out into the world reflects back on us, drawing people, opportunities, and success that resonate with our deepest intentions.

The journey towards more authentic engagement is not just about changing tactics but about embracing a more profound transformation in how we view the act of doing business. It's a path that champions simplicity, honors the individual, and celebrates the connections that enrich both our personal and professional lives. In this light, success is not measured solely by sales or metrics but by the depth and quality of the relationships we forge along the way. It's a testament to the idea that when we lead with love and integrity, what we seek is indeed seeking us.

The pains you feel are messengers.

Listen to them.

In the complex landscape of customer service, complaints often appear as unwelcome storms, darkening the rapport between businesses and their clientele. Yet, within every critique lies a golden opportunity, a beacon guiding us towards improvement and innovation. Understanding and embracing customer feedback, particularly complaints, as invaluable gifts can transform the very foundation of how a business evolves to meet the needs of those it serves. This perspective shift is not merely about damage control but about recognizing each complaint as a unique insight into the customer's experience, offering a clear direction for where to focus improvement efforts.

Leading from love, the process of reflecting on customer complaints becomes an act of genuine care and commitment to excellence. It's an opportunity to dig deeply into the heart of our service or product, identifying not just the superficial fixes but the root causes that led to dissatisfaction. This approach fosters a culture of openness and continuous learning, where feedback is not feared but welcomed as a guide towards becoming better. It requires a balance of humility and confidence, to listen actively and respond not defensively but with a desire to understand and improve.

Treating complaints as gifts encourages a deeper connection with our customers. It shows that their voices are heard, their concerns are taken seriously, and their satisfaction is paramount. This level of engagement builds trust and loyalty, laying the groundwork for a relationship that goes beyond transactional interactions to one of mutual respect and appreciation. It's a testament to the business's commitment to not just meeting but exceeding customer expectations, continually refining its offerings to reflect the desires and needs of those it aims to serve.

Additionally, this mindset shifts towards embracing feedback is a powerful driver of innovation. It challenges us to look beyond the status quo, to question our assumptions, and to see our services through the eyes of those we serve. By doing so, we open the door to creative solutions that may not have been apparent from within the confines of conventional thinking. It's an invitation to engage in a dynamic, ongoing dialogue with our customers, co-creating experiences that delight and inspire.

The journey of embracing customer complaints as gifts is a profound one, leading to not just incremental improvements but to a transformative shift in how a business understands and interacts with its customers. It's about cultivating a culture that sees feedback as a precious resource, illuminating the path towards excellence. By approaching each complaint with empathy, curiosity, and a commitment to growth, businesses can turn challenges into opportunities, deepening their connection with customers and paving the way for lasting success and innovation.

It is difficult to convey the magic of love

to those who are made of dust.

In the journey of leadership and innovation, one of the most profound challenges we face is communicating the essence of our vision – a vision often born from a place of deep passion and love – to those who may not readily see its value. This difficulty stems not from a lack of eloquence or clarity but from the intrinsic nature of transformational ideas: they require not just understanding but belief, a leap of faith that not everyone is prepared to make. It's an endeavor that tests the limits of our ability to inspire, to connect, and to evoke a sense of possibility in others.

Leading from love, we are guided by the recognition that true connection and understanding go beyond the mere exchange of ideas. It involves reaching into the depths of our own conviction and authenticity, to find ways to bridge the gap between what is and what could be. This process is not about diluting our vision to make it more palatable but about finding the language, the stories, and the shared experiences that can illuminate its essence for others.

This challenge is particularly poignant in environments resistant to change, where the prevailing mindset is anchored in the 'dust' of conventional wisdom and established practices. Here, the task of the leader is to awaken a sense of curiosity and openness, to gently challenge and guide others towards a broader perspective. It requires a blend of leadership to navigate the nuances of human resistance, mutual love and care to foster an environment where new ideas can be explored without fear, and an unwavering commitment to the transformative power of the vision itself.

The journey of sharing our vision is as much about our own growth as it is about inspiring change in others. It tests our resilience, our empathy, and our ability to lead with a heart full of love, even when faced with indifference or skepticism. It is a reminder that the magic of love, the driving force behind our most daring dreams and visions, is not something to be forced but shared with patience, understanding, and the hope that it will eventually find fertile ground.

The endeavor to convey the magic of our vision to those who are not immediately receptive is a profound exercise in leadership, empathy, and faith. It challenges us to remain steadfast in our convictions while being open to the myriad ways in which our message can be understood and embraced. It is a journey that underscores the beauty of striving to connect, to share, and to transform, grounded in the knowledge that, though not everyone may see the magic at first, the effort to illuminate it is itself an act of love and optimism.

I do not waste my words on tired minds,

I can only talk to those you are thirsty for the sea.

Leading from love means seeking out those who are thirsty for the sea of possibilities, those who believe in the potential for a brighter future and are willing to embrace simplicity and ease. It's about surrounding yourself with individuals who uplift and inspire, who see challenges as opportunities and believe in the power of positive change.

Simplicity is the key idea that guides this approach. By focusing on the essential and stripping away unnecessary complications, we can create a path that is both clear and achievable. Simplicity allows us to cut through the noise and concentrate on what truly matters, fostering an environment where innovation and growth can flourish.

In the workplace, this mindset fosters a culture of optimism and resilience. When we choose to engage with those who have a positive outlook, we create a supportive and motivating atmosphere. This environment encourages creativity and collaboration, as team members feel empowered to share their ideas and take bold steps toward their goals.

Balancing emotional, intellectual, and spiritual elements is crucial in this journey. Emotionally, it means cultivating a positive mindset and maintaining a sense of hope and possibility. Intellectually, it involves applying clear and logical thinking to simplify processes and make effective decisions. Spiritually, it's about connecting with a higher purpose and believing in the potential for a better future.

This approach transforms how we handle challenges. Instead of being bogged down by negativity and doubt, we embrace a proactive stance, seeking solutions and opportunities for growth. By focusing on simplicity, we make it easier to navigate through difficulties and find creative ways to overcome obstacles.

In practice, this means creating systems and processes that prioritize simplicity and efficiency. Agile methodologies, for instance, emphasize iterative progress and flexibility, allowing teams to adapt quickly and effectively. By integrating these principles, organizations can build a dynamic and responsive environment where simplicity and ease are at the forefront.

Engaging with those who share this vision of simplicity and positivity also enhances interconnectedness. When people feel supported and valued, they are more likely to take risks and innovate. This sense of safety fosters a culture of trust and openness, where everyone is encouraged to contribute their best ideas and efforts.

Choosing to surround ourselves with those who believe in simplicity and ease creates a ripple effect of positive change. It inspires us to see the potential in every situation and to approach our work and lives with a sense of purpose and joy. This path, guided by love and simplicity, leads to a future where challenges are met with confidence and optimism, and where success is achieved through clarity and focus.

Travel brings power and love back into your life.

In the bustling corridors of business, where the glow of screens often outshines the light of day, there lies a transformative power in the act of stepping beyond our familiar confines. It is in the journey towards the spaces inhabited by our customers, suppliers, and even our competitors, that we rediscover the vitality and love that fuel our ambitions and dreams. This venture, though it may span mere miles, has the profound ability to infuse our professional lives with renewed energy and perspective, reminding us of the interconnected human essence at the heart of every transaction and strategy.

Leading from love, we recognize that each interaction, each visit, is an opportunity to not only understand but to connect on a deeper level with the people who are integral to our business's ecosystem. It's a practice that transcends the traditional dynamics of commerce, elevating our relationships from mere contracts and negotiations to genuine bonds forged in mutual respect and understanding. In this act of reaching out, of seeking to know and be known, we find ourselves not just gathering insights but making connections that can support and enrich our business in immeasurable ways.

This approach is a testament to the balance between the emotional and intellectual, between the tangible metrics of success and the intangible value of human connection. It encourages a leadership style that is not just informed by data but is also guided by empathy, intuition, and the genuine desire to make a positive impact. In doing so, we not only enhance our capacity for innovation and adaptability but also foster an environment of care and trust, both within our teams and in our wider business relationships.

The journey beyond our office walls serves as a powerful reminder of the love that initially inspired us to embark on our business venture. It rekindles the passion that can sometimes be dimmed by routine and challenges, reigniting our commitment to our work and the people it touches. This love, coupled with the power derived from truly engaging with our community, propels us towards greater heights of creativity, service, and fulfillment.

The act of venturing out to meet face-to-face with those who shape the world of our business is not merely a strategy for growth; it is a celebration of the human spirit, a journey that brings power and love back into our lives. It reminds us that at the core of every business endeavor lies the opportunity for connection, learning, and, ultimately, transformation – both for ourselves and for the world we aim to serve.

Dance, when you're broken open.

Dance, if you've torn the bandage off.

Dance in the middle of the fighting.

Dance in your blood.

Dance when you're perfectly free.

In the ebb and flow of life and business, we are often faced with moments that test our resilience, challenge our convictions, and sometimes leave us feeling as though we stand amidst the rubble of our plans and dreams. Yet, it is within these very moments that we are presented with a profound choice: to succumb to despair or to embrace the situation with a heart full of love, finding the strength to dance amidst the turmoil.

Leading from love, we find the courage to face each moment as it comes, not with resignation, but with a spirit of acceptance and the determination to move forward. This choice, to dance in the face of adversity, is not a denial of pain or challenge but an affirmation of life and the capacity for joy and growth in every circumstance. It is a testament to the indomitable human spirit, to the resilience that lies within each of us, beckoning us to rise, to heal, and to find freedom in the very act of embracing our present reality with love.

The dance, metaphorical though it may be, symbolizes a celebration of existence in all its facets – joyous and painful, triumphant and trying. It represents a state of being that transcends the immediate challenges, reaching into the depths of our being to tap into a wellspring of love and strength that fuels our journey. It is in this dance that we find the grace to be vulnerable, to express our true selves, and to connect with others in a way that is raw, real, and rich with possibility.

This approach resonates deeply with the principles of holistic well-being. It encourages us to lead with empathy, to cultivate environments where every member feels seen and supported, and to approach our personal and professional relationships with a balance of emotional, intellectual, and spiritual awareness. It is a reminder that the true essence of leadership lies not in stoicism or detachment but in the ability to be fully present, fully human, and fully engaged with the moment, even – especially – when it challenges us.

The invitation to dance, regardless of our circumstances, is an invitation to live and lead from a place of love. It is a call to embrace each moment with all its complexities and to find within ourselves the strength and the freedom to navigate the journey with grace, resilience, and an open heart. It is a testament to the power of love to transform not just our own experiences but to inspire those around us to find their own dance, their own expression of love and freedom, no matter what the situation may hold.

when someone beats a rug,

the blows are not against the rug,

but against the dust in it.

In the intricate ecosystem of an organization, performance challenges are not uncommon. Yet, the manner in which these challenges are addressed can profoundly impact the culture, morale, and future success of the entity. It's a delicate art, akin to removing dust from a cherished rug, where the focus must be on purifying the process, not chastising the fabric that holds the organization together. This perspective shift, from blaming to understanding and improving, marks the difference between a team that emerges stronger from adversity and one that frays at the edges.

Leading from love, we recognize that each individual within the organization is an integral piece of the larger story of its mission and values. When performance issues arise, it's an invitation to examine the processes and systems that guide our actions and decisions. It's a call to identify the dust – the inefficiencies, the misalignments, the outdated practices – that has settled over time, obscuring the vibrant potential of the team.

Addressing these challenges requires a leadership approach that is grounded in empathy, clarity, and a commitment to collective growth. It involves engaging the team in open, honest dialogues where feedback is welcomed and valued, not feared. This approach fosters a culture of connection, where individuals feel empowered to share their insights and ideas, knowing that their contributions will be met with respect and consideration.

This process-oriented perspective encourages a mindset of continuous improvement, where agility, innovation, and collaboration are the driving forces. It's about creating an environment where learning from setbacks is as celebrated as achieving milestones, where the journey of refinement and adaptation is part of the organization's DNA.

When we view performance challenges as opportunities to cleanse and rejuvenate our processes, we affirm the inherent value and potential of our people. We shift the narrative from one of fault and failure to one of growth and possibility. It's a leadership ethos that recognizes the difference between the dust and the rug, between the temporary obstacles that cloud our path and the enduring strength of our team. By focusing our efforts on clearing away the dust, we not only enhance our performance but also deepen our connections, reinforce our values, and illuminate the way forward with renewed clarity and purpose. In doing so, we embody the true essence of leading with love, compassion, and a steadfast belief in the potential of our people and our organization.

Love will find its way through all languages on its own.

In a world where the language of business is often dominated by metrics, targets, and bottom lines, there exists a more profound, universal language that transcends words and numbers: the language of love. When a business truly centers itself around meeting the needs of its customers, this commitment manifests itself naturally across every interaction, every product, and every service. It's a language that customers understand intuitively, a signal that they are valued and understood, not just as consumers, but as human beings.

Leading from love, a business crafts not just transactions but relationships. This ethos becomes the north star, guiding every decision, every innovation, and every form of communication. It's a principle that permeates the organization's culture, influencing not only how team members interact with customers but also how they collaborate and support one another. In such an environment, empathy, understanding, and genuine care become the defining characteristics, fostering a sense of community and connection that customers can feel deeply.

This approach transcends the conventional strategies of customer service, entering the territory of true customer engagement and loyalty. It's about understanding that at the heart of every business exchange lies an opportunity to touch a life, to make a difference, and to forge a bond that goes beyond the superficial. When love guides a business's actions, it creates a resonance that is unmistakable, a vibe that customers are drawn to and want to be a part of.

This commitment to operating from a place of love and empathy naturally aligns with the principles of human-centered design. These principles become not just strategies but reflections of the organization's core values, woven into the very fabric of its operations. It's a holistic approach that recognizes the importance of every touchpoint, from the first contact to post-purchase support, as an opportunity to communicate love and respect for the customer.

When a business is genuinely focused on embracing and meeting the needs of its customers, it speaks the universal language of love fluently and effortlessly. This language, understood by all, becomes the most potent tool in a business's arsenal, capable of breaking down barriers, building trust, and creating lasting relationships. It's a reminder that in the end, the most successful businesses are those that lead with love, recognizing that it is not just an emotion but a powerful force that can transform interactions, relationships, and even entire organizations.

Listen with ears of tolerance!

See through the eyes of compassion!

Speak with the language of love.

In a world clamoring for attention, where voices often rise in a cacophony of opinions, demands, and narratives, the act of truly listening, observing, and then speaking emerges not just as a skill, but as a profound act of love and respect. This sequence – listen, observe, speak – is a dance of engagement that transcends the superficial layers of interaction, touching the very essence of human connection. It is a practice that requires us to set aside our egos, our preconceptions, and our agendas, to truly be present with another.

Leading from love, we approach each conversation with the openness to truly hear what is being said, beyond the words. Listening with ears of tolerance allows us to embrace a multitude of perspectives, even those that challenge our own. This kind of listening is not passive; it is an active, deliberate choice to engage with the world from a place of empathy and curiosity. It is the first step in a journey toward understanding and connection, a foundation upon which trust is built and from which genuine relationships can grow.

Observation follows, a practice of seeing through eyes of compassion. Here, we engage not just with our senses but with our hearts, recognizing the humanity in each other. This form of observation seeks to understand the emotions, intentions, and unspoken truths that lie beneath the surface. It is a reminder that every person we encounter carries their own stories, struggles, and dreams. By observing with compassion, we honor those stories, creating a space where individuals feel valued and understood.

Finally, to speak with the language of love is to choose words that heal, uplift, and inspire. It is to recognize the power of our language to shape realities and to use that power with intention and grace. This language does not shy away from truth but delivers it with kindness, acknowledging that our words have the ability to impact the hearts and minds of those around us. In choosing to speak from a place of love, we contribute to a culture of positivity, encouragement, and mutual support.

This sequence of listening, observing, and speaking, grounded in love, tolerance, and compassion, represents a fundamental shift in how we interact with the world. It challenges us to move beyond transactional exchanges, fostering instead a deeper level of engagement and understanding. In doing so, we not only enrich our own lives but also touch the lives of others, contributing to a collective environment where growth, connection, and love can flourish. This is the incredible gift of love we offer each other, a gift that transforms both giver and receiver, and ultimately, the world around us.

If love were only spiritual, the practices of fasting
and prayer would not exist.

In the intricate dance of the workplace, where the tangible meets the intangible, our daily practices and rituals serve as a profound testament to the culture of love, safety, and well-being. Rumi's wisdom invites us to consider that the essence of love transcends the purely spiritual; it demands expression through our actions and interactions, through the very fabric of our communal life at work.

Leading from love, we recognize that the routines and ceremonies we establish within our organizations are not mere tasks or checkboxes. They are, instead, the physical manifestations of our collective values, a way of embodying and reinforcing a culture where every individual feels valued, understood, and protected. These practices, ranging from how we greet each other to the structure of our meetings, and even to the rituals of recognition and celebration, are the connecting threads of a healthy and vibrant workplace.

This approach underscores the significance of human awareness in shaping an environment where safety and well-being are paramount. It calls for leaders and team members alike to cultivate an awareness of and responsiveness to the emotional currents that flow through our workspaces. By fostering an atmosphere of leading from love, we create a space where individuals can express themselves freely, share ideas without fear, and contribute to a collective resilience and creativity.

The principles of self-management offer frameworks for operationalizing these values within the structural and procedural dimensions of our work. These methodologies, with their emphasis on flexibility, collaboration, and shared governance, reflect a commitment to practices that are not only effective but deeply human-centered. They enable us to design systems and processes that honor the dignity of each person and the interconnectedness of our efforts.

The daily ceremonies of work – be they the rhythms of collaboration, the rituals of feedback and reflection, or the celebrations of milestones achieved – are expressions of a deeper commitment to cultivating a workplace anchored in love, safety, and growth. They remind us that the quality of our collective life at work is measured not only by outcomes and outputs but by the depth of care, connection, and respect we bring to our shared journey.

As we move forward, let us embrace the wisdom that love's true power is revealed not just in what we feel but in what we do. By weaving love into the very practices and ceremonies of our work, we not only enrich our immediate environment but contribute to a broader culture of kindness, innovation, and well-being that resonates far beyond the walls of our workplaces.

Lovers find secret places in this violent world
where they make transactions with beauty.

In the often tumultuous landscape of modern commerce, where transactions are marked by competition and self-interest, there exists the potential for a different kind of interaction – one marked by vulnerability, transparency, and mutual respect. Drawing inspiration from the power of love, businesses and their partners can create sanctuaries of beauty in their dealings, where sincerity replaces suspicion, and collaboration supersedes contention.

Leading from love, we find that the most enduring and fruitful relationships between customers and suppliers are those rooted in honesty and open communication. This approach not only humanizes the commercial exchange but elevates it to a partnership where both parties are invested in each other's success. It's a shift from seeing transactions as zero-sum games to viewing them as opportunities for mutual growth and enrichment.

This ethos of vulnerability and transparency is supported by a foundation of human awareness, which allows for a deeper understanding and connection between people in a business context. It encourages an environment where challenges are faced together, solutions are co-created, and successes are shared. This level of engagement fosters trust, loyalty, and a sense of shared purpose, transforming routine transactions into meaningful exchanges that contribute to a larger narrative of cooperation and progress.

The principles of Agile, Sociocracy, and Holacracy provide practical frameworks for implementing these ideals into the organizational structure and processes. These methodologies advocate for flexibility, distributed authority, and open dialogue, which align with the ethos of conducting business from a place of love and mutual respect. They offer a blueprint for creating work environments that not only embrace but thrive on transparency and collaboration.

The journey toward more human-centered and compassionate business practices is one of profound transformation. It requires us to reconsider the foundations upon which our commercial relationships are built and to reimagine them as partnerships characterized by depth, understanding, and a shared commitment to beauty in all its forms. This approach not only enhances the immediate business outcomes but contributes to a broader cultural shift towards empathy, sustainability, and collective well-being.

By choosing to engage each other on terms of vulnerability and transparency, customers and suppliers can co-create spaces of tranquility and beauty amid the chaos of the commercial world. It is a testament to the power of love to inspire change, to transform transactions into partnerships, and to remind us that at the heart of every business endeavor lies the potential for connection, growth, and mutual flourishing.

Love is not love that doesn't love the details of the
beloved, the minute particulars.

In the intricate dance of running a business, it's often the whisper of the minutiae that orchestrates success. While grand visions and bold strategies sketch the outline of progress, it's the attention to the smallest details that colors in the picture, bringing it to vibrant life. This meticulous care for every aspect of our operations is where the true heart of a business beats. It is a testament to the love we hold not just for our enterprise but for the people it serves and the teams that fuel it. To cherish the details is to honor the trust placed in us by every customer, every employee, every partner.

Leading from love, we begin to see that the minutiae are not mere tasks or checkboxes but the very essence of our connection to our work and to each other. It's in the way we listen to a customer's feedback, noticing not just the words but the emotion behind them. It's in the care we take in crafting an email, choosing our words to resonate not just with clarity but with empathy. This approach transforms routine operations into acts of kindness, making every small decision a reflection of our broader commitment to excellence and to each other.

Imagine a business environment where every detail is infused with this spirit of care and attention. This is a place where simplicity is not just a design principle but a way of being, where the innocence of our intentions shines through in the clarity of our actions. It's a space where the balance between the emotional, the intellectual, and the spiritual is maintained not through effort but through instinct, guided by a leadership that sees the value in every contribution, no matter how small.

In such a culture, the principles of agility and innovation are not just applied to products and services but to the very fabric of organizational life. Here, strategic intuition guides decision-making, mutual respect encourages open dialogue, and a human-centered approach shapes every strategy and system. It's a setting where the power of attraction – drawing towards us what we focus on with love and attention – manifests not just in personal growth but in business success.

This deep focus on the particulars, this devotion to the details, is what elevates a company from good to extraordinary. It's a recognition that in the complex system of business, every thread counts, every color has its place, and the beauty of the whole depends on the love we pour into every single stitch. By embracing this philosophy, we create businesses that are not just successful but soulful, not just efficient but beloved.

I have been a seeker and I still am,

but I stopped asking the books and the stars.

I started listening to the teaching of my soul.

In the relentless pursuit of success and understanding in the business world, there comes a pivotal moment when external guides, no matter how insightful, reach the limits of their influence. The true compass, capable of navigating the intricate dynamics of leadership and innovation, lies within the quiet, steady voice of our inner selves. This internal advisor, forged from the depths of our experiences, emotions, and the very essence of who we are, speaks in whispers of intuition and insight. When we learn to quiet the noise of the outside world and tune into this inner guidance, we unlock a reservoir of wisdom far more attuned to our unique journey than any consultant or strategy could ever offer.

Leading from love, we embark on a transformative journey towards authentic leadership and decision-making. It's a path that recognizes the power of aligning our actions with the core of our being, where the clarity and conviction found in the silence of our own soul outshine the brightest stars and the most learned books. This alignment allows us to navigate the complexities of our roles with an ease and authenticity that inspires those around us, cultivating an environment where trust, innovation, and resilience flourish.

Imagine a workplace where leaders and team members alike are encouraged to cultivate this deep connection to their inner wisdom. In this space, the simplicity of being true to yourself guides complex decision-making, and the innocence of genuine intent enhances the integrity of our actions. Here, the balance between rational thought and intuitive insights is seamlessly maintained, creating a fertile ground for innovation and growth. This environment thrives on the premise that the most profound insights often come from within, encouraging a culture of introspection and continuous personal growth.

Such a culture not only elevates the individual but also transforms the collective, fostering a community where the wisdom of each person's soul contributes to an energy of collective intelligence and empathy. It's a place where the harmony between personal intuition and collaborative effort guides the organization towards its highest aspirations, making the workplace not just a site of economic activity but a sanctuary of shared human experience and discovery.

By honoring the teachings of our souls, we tap into a wellspring of guidance that is both profoundly personal and universally applicable. This approach transcends the traditional reliance on external expertise, inviting us instead to trust in the inherent wisdom that resides within each of us. It is here, in the sacred space of inner knowing, that we find the most powerful advisor of all, guiding us not just towards success, but towards a deeper, more fulfilling expression of our work and ourselves.

If you look too closely at the form,

you'll miss the essence.

In the intricate dance of business, where processes and systems serve as the backbone of success, there lies a subtle truth often overshadowed by the pursuit of perfection. Each moment in the life of a business is unique, filled with its own set of challenges and opportunities. It's a dynamic landscape where the quest for flawless execution can sometimes lead us astray, focusing our gaze so intently on the minutiae that we lose sight of the broader horizon. The beauty of any process lies not in its unattainable perfection but in the engagement of the people who navigate it and in the outcomes they create.

Leading from love, we begin to see the workplace not as a factory of flawless outputs but as a garden of growth and discovery. This perspective allows us to appreciate the efforts of those around us, to celebrate the journey as much as the destination. It acknowledges that while the paths we take may be fraught with imperfections, they are also ripe with opportunities for learning, innovation, and connection. By embracing this mindset, we cultivate an environment where every misstep is a stepping stone to greater understanding and every achievement is a testament to the resilience and creativity of our teams.

Such an approach requires a shift from a culture of criticism to one of curiosity and compassion. It encourages us to ask not only how we can improve our processes but also how we can enhance the experiences of those who contribute to them. It's about recognizing that the essence of our work lies not in the rigid adherence to procedures but in the collective spirit of those who carry them out. This spirit, fueled by a shared sense of purpose and commitment, is what ultimately drives our businesses forward.

Embracing the imperfection of processes does not mean settling for mediocrity; rather, it's about acknowledging the inherent unpredictability of business and the human reality at its core. It's a celebration of engagement over efficiency, of meaning over mechanics. In doing so, we not only achieve more humane and sustainable outcomes but also forge deeper connections with our work and with each other.

The journey of any business is a mosaic of moments, each imperfect in its own right but collectively forming a picture of progress and purpose. By focusing less on the form and more on the essence, we unlock a more fulfilling and effective way of working – one that honors the contributions of our people, embraces the beauty of our outcomes, and navigates the imperfections of our processes with grace and gratitude.

when setting out on a journey,

do not seek advice from those

who have never left home.

In the exhilarating paths of entrepreneurship and business innovation, every venture embarked upon is a journey into the unknown. The path is often uncharted, the challenges unforeseen, and the rewards uncertain. In such a landscape, guidance and wisdom become invaluable commodities. However, the source of such advice is as critical as the advice itself. The marketplace is teeming with coaches and consultants eager to offer their strategies and solutions, each promising the key to success. Yet, true wisdom – the kind that leads to genuine breakthroughs and enduring success – often comes from those who have navigated their own unique journeys, who have faced the tempests and charted their own courses through turbulent waters.

Leading from love, the importance of seeking guidance from those with firsthand experience becomes even more pronounced. It's about connecting with individuals who have not only theorized about paths to success but have walked those paths themselves. These are the mentors and advisors who understand that the fabric of business success is woven from threads of trial, error, and resilience. Their advice is grounded in real-world experiences, imbued with the depth of understanding that comes from having navigated the complexities and nuances of launching and growing a business.

This approach to seeking advice does not diminish the value of theoretical knowledge or the insights of those who study the mechanics of business success from the outside. However, it places a premium on experiential wisdom, on the learnings that emerge from real-life challenges and victories. It's a recognition that the most profound lessons often come from the scars of battle, not the safety of the sidelines.

Aligning yourself with mentors who have experienced the highs and lows of the entrepreneurial journey fosters a deeper connection to the emotional, intellectual, and spiritual aspects of business leadership. It's about more than just strategies and bottom lines. It is about embracing the journey with all its uncertainties and discovering the strength and creativity within to navigate through them. These mentors not only offer practical advice but also inspire a sense of possibility and courage, reinforcing the belief that with perseverance and passion, any challenge can be overcome.

The journey of business is as much about the internal growth of the entrepreneur as it is about external achievements. By seeking out those who have truly walked the path, who have felt the weight of decisions and the thrill of breakthroughs, we equip ourselves not just with strategies for success, but with the wisdom to thrive amidst the unpredictability of the business landscape. It's a journey best navigated with the guidance of those who know the way not just in theory, but in practice – a testament to the power of experience in shaping leaders who can inspire, innovate, and lead with integrity.

Raise your words, not your voice.

It is rain that grows flowers, not thunder.

In the bustling ecosystems of our workplaces, where the exchange of ideas and the clash of egos often collide, the power of our words becomes ever more evident. The way we communicate – whether drenched in love or laced with frustration – sets the tone for the environment we cultivate and the relationships we build. It's a subtle yet profound realization that the essence of truly effective leadership and collaboration lies not in the volume of our voices but in the quality and intention behind our words. Like the gentle yet persistent rain that nourishes the earth and coaxes flowers to bloom, thoughtful and compassionate communication fosters growth, understanding, and connection among teams.

Leading from love, we understand that to inspire, to motivate, and to guide, our words must resonate with the same frequency as our hearts. This approach to communication goes beyond mere semantics or strategies. It is about embodying a presence that encourages openness, trust, and mutual care. In such an environment, every individual feels valued and heard, paving the way for innovation, creativity, and genuine collaboration. It's here, in this space of mutual respect and empathy, that the true magic of teamwork is realized.

Imagine a workplace where conversations are imbued with the simplicity of clear intentions, the love for shared goals, and the innocence of expressing vulnerabilities without fear. In this haven, the logos, ethos, and pathos of our interactions weave a strong fabric of communal ties, where the balance between listening and speaking is harmoniously maintained. This culture champions the principles of human-centered design, recognizing that at the core of all organizational success are the individuals who bring their unique perspectives, skills, and passions to the table.

Such an environment not only nurtures the well-being of its people but also elevates the collective output to levels beyond the sum of its parts. It's a testament to the fact that when we choose to raise our words with intention and care, rather than our voices in frustration, we create a climate where everyone can thrive. This mindful approach to communication draws upon the timeless wisdom that true influence is born from empathy and understanding, not force or fear.

By embracing this philosophy, we not only transform our workplaces but also contribute to a larger shift in how success is defined and achieved. It's a journey that asks us to be mindful of the tone and style of our words, for it is in this mindfulness that we find the keys to building a legacy of love, growth, and collective achievement. In doing so, we don't just change the narrative of our organizations; we change the world, one word at a time.

If you are irritated by every rub,

how will your mirror be polished?

Embracing tensions and irritations at work as invitations to grow and develop transforms how we perceive challenges. These moments, often seen as obstacles, are opportunities to polish our inner mirrors, revealing the clarity and brilliance within.

Leading from love means understanding that the friction we encounter is a catalyst for growth. It's about recognizing that every challenge holds the potential to refine us, to bring out our best qualities, and to deepen our understanding. This perspective encourages us to welcome difficulties with open hearts and minds, seeing them not as hindrances but as essential elements of our personal and professional development.

Simplicity is the key idea that illuminates this journey. By focusing on the essential lessons within each tension, we strip away unnecessary complexities and distractions. This clarity allows us to see the true value in our experiences, enabling us to learn and grow with intention and purpose. Simplicity helps us navigate through challenges with grace and wisdom, turning irritations into opportunities for profound transformation.

In the workplace, this mindset fosters an environment where psychological safety thrives. When team members feel secure and valued, they are more likely to view challenges as shared opportunities for growth. This collective resilience builds a culture of trust and collaboration, where everyone is committed to learning and evolving together.

Balancing the emotional, intellectual, and spiritual aspects of our responses to challenges enriches our ability to grow. Emotionally, it means acknowledging and embracing our feelings without being overwhelmed by them. Intellectually, it involves analyzing situations to understand the underlying causes and lessons. Spiritually, it's about connecting with a higher purpose, seeing each challenge as part of a greater journey toward self-actualization and fulfillment.

In practice, this approach transforms how we address tensions and irritations. Instead of reacting with frustration or avoidance, we engage with curiosity and compassion. We ask ourselves what each situation is teaching us, how we can grow from it, and how it can bring us closer to our true potential. This proactive stance turns challenges into opportunities, each one polishing our mirror a little more.

At work, this means creating processes and environments that support continuous improvement and learning. Agile methodologies, for example, emphasize iterative progress and adaptability, allowing teams to respond to challenges dynamically. By fostering a culture that values learning over perfection, we encourage innovation and resilience, turning every rub into an opportunity for growth.

Sources of Concepts and Methods

The following concepts and methods have been highly influential on the author and on the creation of this book.

Psychological Safety

Psychological safety is a foundational element in creating environments where individuals feel secure to express themselves without fear of negative consequences. It is crucial for fostering open communication, creativity, and innovation within teams and organizations. When psychological safety is prioritized, it leads to stronger collaboration and trust, allowing people to engage fully and authentically. In the context of leading from love, psychological safety enables a culture of mutual respect and empathy, where everyone's contributions are valued and encouraged.

Learn more: https://amycedmondson.com/psychological-safety/

Leadership Transformation

The Enablers Network has been a driving force in integrating Aristotle's principles of 'Logos, Ethos, and Pathos' into corporate transformation. Their work emphasizes the importance of balancing logic, values, and emotional connections in leadership. By combining these elements, leaders can create environments that are not only effective but also deeply humane. This approach resonates with the idea of leading from love, where authenticity and empathy are central to inspiring and guiding others. Chris Parker, a member of the network, contributes as a coach and trainer on large-scale transformation programs.

Learn more: https://enablersnetwork.com/

Team Growing and Learning

Adjugo's expertise in team coaching and autonomous teams has redefined how organizations approach coaching and training. Their emphasis on flexibility, collaboration, and continuous improvement aligns with the values of leading from love, as it promotes a culture where teams work together harmoniously with a shared purpose. Adjugo's approach fosters environments where individuals are empowered to take initiative and responsibility, leading to greater innovation and success. Chris Parker engages with Adjugo on cultural transformation projects.

Learn more: https://adjugo.com/

Positive Psychology

Positive psychology focuses on the strengths and virtues that enable individuals and communities to thrive. This field of study is essential for understanding how to cultivate happiness, resilience, and a sense of purpose in life. By emphasizing positive emotions and well-being, positive psychology aligns with the principles of leading from love, encouraging a mindset that nurtures personal growth and fulfillment. It serves as a reminder that focusing on the good in ourselves and others can lead to more meaningful and joyful lives.

Learn more: https://positivepsychology.com/

Meditation and Mindfulness

Mindfulness has significantly transformed our understanding and practice of meditation in the modern world, highlighting its profound impact on mental and physical well-being. In Amsterdam, Wineke van Aken has been pivotal in bringing the benefits of mindfulness to a wider audience, guiding individuals in practices that cultivate awareness, presence, and compassion in their everyday lives. Through her work, she helps people connect deeply with themselves and navigate life with greater clarity and inner peace.

Learn more: https://mettamind.nl/

Meditation and Healing

Dr. Joe Dispenza's work on the science of meditation offers profound insights into how meditation can be used for healing and personal transformation. His teachings explore the connection between mind and body, showing how our thoughts and emotions can influence our physical health. Dr. Dispenza's approach brings the timeless wisdom of "what would love do?" into a modern context, providing practical tools for harnessing the power of meditation to create positive change in our lives.

Learn more: https://drjoedispenza.com/

Dr. Joe Dispenza's NeuroChange Solutions program integrates neuroscience and practical strategies to empower individuals and organizations to rewire their brains for higher levels of performance, creativity, and well-being, demonstrating how changing our thoughts and emotions can lead to transformative personal and professional growth.

Learn more: https://neurochangesolutions.com/

Meditation & Self-Love

Esther Hicks, through the teachings of Abraham, emphasizes the importance of meditation and the emotional guidance system as tools for cultivating self-love and inner peace. Her work highlights the power of aligning with our true desires and emotions, teaching that self-love is the foundation for a fulfilled life. By integrating meditation into our daily practice, we can connect with our inner being and make choices that reflect the highest expression of love.

Learn more: https://www.abraham-hicks.com/

Distributed Governance

Holacracy.org promotes a self-managing organizational model that decentralizes authority and empowers individuals at all levels. This distributed governance system replaces traditional hierarchies with flexible, role-based structures that allow for greater autonomy and responsiveness. By fostering an environment where everyone has a voice, Holacracy supports the principles of leading from love, creating organizations that are agile, inclusive, and aligned with their core values.

Learn more: https://www.holacracy.org/

Collaborative Governance

Sociocracy is a collaborative governance system that prioritizes equality, transparency, and shared decision-making. Decisions are made through a consent-based process, ensuring that all voices are heard and respected. Sociocracy's emphasis on participative management aligns with the values of leading from love, as it nurtures a culture of collaboration, mutual respect, and shared responsibility, where the collective wisdom of the group guides the organization's direction.

Learn more: https://sociocracy30.org/

Sustainability

Qhuba's simplicity approach to sustainability offers a clear and effective strategy for achieving long-term goals. By focusing on straightforward and practical solutions, Qhuba advocates for sustainable practices that are both impactful and manageable. This approach is in harmony with leading from love, as it encourages thoughtful decision-making that considers the well-being of both people and the planet, ensuring that sustainability efforts are meaningful and enduring. Chris Parker collaborates with Qhuba on interactive workshops and sustainability interventions.

Learn more: https://qhuba.com/

Human-Centered Design

Human-Centered Design (HCD) is a problem-solving approach that places people at the center of the design process. By deeply understanding the needs, preferences, and experiences of users, HCD ensures that solutions are both functional and meaningful. This methodology aligns with the principles of leading from love, as it emphasizes empathy, creativity, and a deep respect for the human experience. By designing with the end user in mind, HCD fosters innovation that truly resonates with and benefits those it serves.

Learn more: https://www.designkit.org/

Simplicity

Ebullient Business Designers specialize in the art of Simple Business Design, a streamlined approach to creating effective and sustainable business models. Their methodology revolves around the Simple Business Design Canvas, a practical tool that helps organizations distill complex ideas into clear, actionable strategies. Through interactive workshops, Ebullient Business Designers guide teams in collaboratively exploring and refining their business concepts, ensuring that every aspect of the design is aligned with the organization's core values and goals. In addition to workshops, they offer executive coaching to support leaders in implementing and sustaining these designs, fostering a culture of simplicity, agility, and purpose-driven growth. This approach embodies the principles of leading from love, as it emphasizes clarity, intentionality, and the human aspect of business, ensuring that strategies are not only effective but also meaningful and empowering for everyone involved.

Learn more: https://ebullient.com/

The Business Simplicity Podcast is available on all popular podcast platforms. Chris Parker regularly interviews experts and leaders about business simplicity leading from love.

Learn more: http://ebullient.com/podcast/

About Translations

Rumi's profound and intricate poetry has been translated and interpreted in various ways over the centuries. Among the earliest and most respected translators are Reynold A. Nicholson and A. J. Arberry. Nicholson, a British orientalist, was one of the first to translate Rumi's works into English in the early 20th century. His translations are noted for their conformity to the original texts, capturing the complexity and depth of Rumi's mystical thought. A. J. Arberry, another distinguished British scholar, continued Nicholson's work with his own translations in the mid-20th century. Arberry's translations are similarly renowned for their accuracy and scholarly rigor, providing a literal rendition of Rumi's Persian verses. Both Nicholson and Arberry's works are invaluable for their close adherence to the original language and meaning, offering readers a direct window into Rumi's world.

In contrast, the late 20th century saw the rise of more interpretative translations, most notably by Coleman Barks. Barks, an American poet, transformed Rumi's poetry into a form that resonates with contemporary audiences. While not a scholar of Persian, Barks collaborated with academic translations to create versions that emphasize the emotional and spiritual essence of Rumi's work. His renditions have made Rumi the most popular poet in the United States, highlighting the universal and timeless nature of Rumi's themes.

Deepak Chopra, the renowned author and spiritual teacher, also contributed to the modern appreciation of Rumi's poetry. Chopra's books, while inspired by Rumi, reflects his own spiritual insights and interpretations. While not a direct translation, Chopra's work captures the essence of Rumi's messages, aligning them with contemporary spiritual practices and philosophies.

In a unique and spiritually enriching collaboration, Deepak Chopra and Madonna joined forces to create the album "A Gift of Love: Deepak & Friends Present Music Inspired by the Love Poems of Rumi." This project brought together Chopra's profound understanding of Rumi's mystical poetry and Madonna's iconic voice and artistic flair. The album features recitations of Rumi's timeless verses by Madonna and other celebrities, accompanied by evocative music that enhances the emotional and spiritual depth of the poetry. This collaboration aimed to make Rumi's wisdom accessible to a broader audience, blending the ancient Sufi mystic's teachings with contemporary artistic expression.

This book, "Lead from Love with Rumi," draws inspiration from the interpretative translations of popular authors like Coleman Barks and Deepak Chopra. These versions of Rumi's poetry are particularly powerful for today's readers because they invoke a deeper connection to contemporary contexts and issues. By focusing on the spiritual and emotional core of Rumi's work, these interpretations make his timeless wisdom accessible and relevant to modern audiences.

It's important to note that the use of modern interpretative translations in this book is not intended to diminish the Islamic foundation of Rumi's work. Instead, it aims to highlight the universal aspects of his teachings. Rumi's poetry, grounded in his faith and Sufi practice, speaks to the human experience in a way that transcends religious and cultural boundaries. The essence of his message – love, connection, and spiritual growth – remains intact, offering guidance and inspiration to leaders today.

By exploring Rumi's teachings through the lens of these modern interpretations, this book seeks to provide a practical and heartfelt approach to leadership. It's an invitation to lead from love, drawing on the profound wisdom of Rumi as translated and interpreted by voices that bridge the past with the present.

The following are sources of Rumi's wisdom:

Jalal ad-Din Muhammad Rumi:

- **Masnavi (Masnavi-i Ma'navi):** Often referred to as the "Spiritual Couplets," this is Rumi's magnum opus and consists of six books of poetry that explore various aspects of spiritual life and human existence. It is considered one of the greatest works of mystical poetry.

- **Divan-e Shams-e Tabrizi (The Collected Poems of Shams of Tabriz):** This is a collection of lyric poems (ghazals) dedicated to Rumi's spiritual teacher, Shams of Tabriz. The collection reflects Rumi's deep emotional and spiritual bond with Shams.
- **Fihi Ma Fihi (In It What's in It):** This is a collection of Rumi's prose lectures and discourses. It provides insights into his thoughts on various philosophical and spiritual topics.
- **Majalis-e Sab'a (Seven Sessions):** This is a collection of seven sermons given by Rumi, covering a range of spiritual and ethical topics.
- **Makatib (The Letters):** This collection consists of Rumi's letters to his disciples, family members, and others. These letters offer a glimpse into Rumi's personal life and his teachings.

It has been difficult to definitively trace the specific English translations to any single source as they have been adapted and interpreted so many times since Rumi originally wrote them. The most common and credible translations and interpretations have been written by the following and the books listed are the most popular books where you can discover even more inspiration.

Reynold A. Nicholson:

- **The Mathnawi of Jalaluddin Rumi:** This is Nicholson's magnum opus, an eight-volume work that provides an English translation of Rumi's "Masnavi," along with extensive commentary and analysis. This translation is one of the most comprehensive and authoritative versions available.

- **Rumi: Poet and Mystic:** This book includes selections from Rumi's "Divan-e Shams-e Tabrizi" and "Masnavi," offering readers a taste of Rumi's poetry and mystical teachings.
- **The Mystics of Islam:** While not exclusively about Rumi, this book includes significant portions of Rumi's work and provides context for understanding his place within the broader tradition of Islamic mysticism.

A. J. Arberry:

- **Tales from the Masnavi:** This book contains a selection of stories from Rumi's "Masnavi," translated into English with an aim to preserve the spirit and wisdom of the original texts.
- **Mystical Poems of Rumi:** In this collection, Arberry translated many of Rumi's poems, capturing the essence of Rumi's mystical insights and lyrical beauty.
- **Discourses of Rumi:** This translation provides English readers with access to Rumi's prose works, particularly his discourses which explore various aspects of Sufi thought and practice.
- **The Rubaiyat of Jalal al-Din Rumi:** Arberry translated a selection of Rumi's quatrains, known as "rubaiyat," which are concise and often profound poetic expressions of Sufi philosophy and spiritual insight.

Coleman Barks:

- **The Essential Rumi:** This is one of Barks' most popular works, offering a comprehensive collection of Rumi's poems that capture the essence of his spiritual and mystical insights.
- **The Soul of Rumi: A New Collection of Ecstatic Poems:** This book features a wide selection of Rumi's poems, emphasizing the themes of love, spirituality, and the human experience.

- **Rumi: The Book of Love:** Poems of Ecstasy and Longing: In this collection, Barks focuses on Rumi's poetry about love, exploring its many dimensions and its central role in Rumi's philosophy.
- **The Illuminated Rumi:** This book pairs Barks' translations of Rumi's poetry with beautiful artwork, creating a visually and spiritually enriching experience for readers.
- **Rumi: Bridge to the Soul:** Journeys into the Music and Silence of the Heart: This collection presents Rumi's poems based on the themes of the soul, music, and the heart, offering readers profound insights into Rumi's mystical vision.
- **A Year with Rumi: Daily Readings:** This book provides readers with a daily dose of Rumi's wisdom, featuring a different poem or excerpt for each day of the year.
- **Rumi: The Big Red Book: The Great Masterpiece Celebrating Mystical Love and Friendship:** This work compiles many of Rumi's most beloved poems, celebrating themes of love, friendship, and spiritual connection.

Deepak Chopra:

- **The Book of Secrets: Unlocking the Hidden Dimensions of Your Life:** While not solely about Rumi, this book incorporates many of Rumi's insights and teachings into Chopra's exploration of spiritual wisdom and personal transformation.
- **The Love Poems of Rumi:** In this book, Chopra provides translations and interpretations of Rumi's poems that focus on the theme of love. This collection aims to bring Rumi's timeless wisdom to a contemporary audience.
- **A Gift of Love - Deepak & Friends Present Music Inspired by the Love Poems of Rumi:** This is an audio CD rather than a book, but it is a notable contribution by Chopra. The CD features recitations of Rumi's poems by various celebrities and includes Chopra's interpretations and reflections.

Additional Sources:

- **Mevlana Celaleddin-i Rumi:** Source of information about Rumi from his own family: https://www.mevlana.net/
- **The Mevlana Museum (Konya, Turkey):** This museum, located in Rumi's final resting place, is one of the most significant sources for understanding Rumi's life and works. It houses many manuscripts, personal artifacts, and documents related to Rumi.
- **The International Mevlana Foundation and The Mevlevi Order:** Also known as the Whirling Dervishes, this Sufi order was founded by Rumi's followers after his death. They continue to preserve and promote his teachings and writings.
- **The Threshold Society:** Provides information on Sufi teachings and includes detailed discussions on Rumi's works, philosophy, and his impact on Sufism: https://sufism.org/
- **Rumi: Rumi Quotes and Rumi Poems:** Outstanding online resource about Rumi: https://www.rumi.org.uk/

About Rumi

Jalāl ad-Dīn Muhammad Rūmī, often simply known as Rumi, was born on September 30, 1207, in the city of Balkh, in what is now Afghanistan. He later moved to Konya, in present-day Turkey, where he spent the majority of his life and where his teachings and poetry would flourish. Rumi's profound influence as a poet, mystic, and theologian continues to resonate across the world, transcending cultural and physical boundaries.

Rumi was born into a family of theologians. His father, Baha' ud-Din Walad, was a respected scholar and mystic. This intellectual and spiritual environment profoundly influenced Rumi's early development. When political unrest forced his family to flee Balkh, they traveled extensively, finally settling in Konya. This journey exposed Rumi to a diverse range of spiritual and cultural influences, shaping his unique perspective on life and spirituality.

A pivotal moment in Rumi's life came in 1244 when he met Shams of Tabriz, a wandering dervish and mystic. Shams became Rumi's spiritual mentor, profoundly transforming his life and work. Their intense, spiritual friendship awakened a deep well of mystical insight and poetry within Rumi. Shams' influence can be seen in Rumi's passionate verses and his emphasis on the transformative power of divine love. The disappearance of Shams, whether by death or departure, led to Rumi's prolific output of poetry, much of which expresses his longing and love for his lost friend and mentor.

Rumi's reputation as a mystic and teacher grew, and he attracted a large following. His teachings emphasized the importance of love, the pursuit of inner knowledge, and the unity of being. Rumi believed that love was the fundamental force connecting all of creation, and he encouraged his followers to seek a direct, personal experience of the divine. As a teacher, Rumi used storytelling, poetry, and dance – most notably the whirling dance of the Mevlevi order, or Whirling Dervishes – to guide his disciples on their spiritual journeys.

Rumi's work centers around the theme of love – divine, passionate, and all-encompassing. His key messages include the importance of inner transformation, the unity of all beings, and the power of love to transcend the mundane and connect us to the divine. He teaches that by embracing love in all its forms, we can overcome our ego, dissolve barriers, and achieve a state of spiritual enlightenment. His poetry often speaks to the heart, encouraging readers to look within and discover the divine presence in everyday life.

'Rumi and Chris' by Jentien ten Heuvel 2024

About the Author

Originally from Los Angeles, California, Chris Parker has spent over half of his life outside the United States. He now calls the Netherlands home, living near Amsterdam. This international experience has shaped Chris's unique perspective on leadership and transformation in a global context.

Professionally, Chris has held pivotal roles in several major organizations. He served as the Chief Information Officer (CIO) for LeasePlan, the largest fleet management company in the world. During his tenure, he drove significant innovations and transformations, helping to establish LeasePlan as a leader in mobility and fleet solutions.

More recently, Chris has taken on the role of Chief Experience Officer for Tactful AI, a leading innovator in omnichannel communications solutions. Here, he focuses on creating holistic product experiences that enhance customer engagement and satisfaction. His work at Tactful AI reflects his commitment to integrating advanced technologies with a human-centric approach.

In addition to his corporate roles, Chris founded Ebullient Business Designers (ebullient.com), which helps leaders simplify their businesses through personal coaching and consulting. The core of his approach is the Simple Business Design framework, which emphasizes clarity, focus, and streamlined processes. The Business Simplicity Podcast is where he shares his insights and engages with leaders and experts from around the world.

Chris's leadership philosophy begins with self-love and is deeply inspired by the works of Abraham Hicks and Dr. Joe Dispenza, as well as the timeless wisdom of Rumi. He believes that understanding and nurturing one's inner self is crucial for leading others effectively. This holistic view of leadership integrates emotional, intellectual, and spiritual dimensions, creating a balanced and compassionate approach.

Coming soon...

LEAD FROM LOVE WITH THE STOICS

You become what you give your attention to.
- EPICTITUS

In the quiet moments of reflection, we often come to understand a profound truth: our lives are shaped by where we place our attention. This concept, rooted deeply in ancient wisdom, teaches us that what we focus on expands. When we give our energy to negativity and toxic behaviors, we find ourselves engulfed by them. Conversely, when we nurture love, compassion, and a sense of wholeness, these qualities flourish within us and around us.

Leading from love means embracing a mindset that transcends the mundane and the superficial. It is about choosing to see the inherent goodness in ourselves and others, even when circumstances might suggest otherwise. This perspective invites us to cultivate an inner garden of positivity and grace, where every thought and action is an act of creation, building a life filled with meaning and purpose.

Imagine your mind as a fertile field. Seeds of negativity and toxicity can quickly grow into thorny brambles, choking out the light and leaving you entangled in despair. Yet, within the same field, seeds of love and compassion have the potential to bloom into vibrant flowers, bringing beauty and harmony. The choice of which seeds to plant, water, and nurture lies within us. By consciously deciding to focus on the positive, we transform our inner and outer worlds.

The path to maintaining this focus is not always straightforward. It requires an awareness of our thoughts and emotions and a commitment to self-awareness and self-regulation. This journey involves balancing the emotional, intellectual, and spiritual aspects of our being, creating a holistic approach to life. By integrating these dimensions, we can navigate challenges with resilience and grace, fostering an environment where psychological safety and emotional intelligence thrive.

In our professional lives, this philosophy can lead to transformative leadership. A leader who embodies love and compassion inspires others to do the same. They create a culture of trust and mutual respect, where individuals feel valued and motivated to contribute their best. Such an environment is not only more harmonious but also more productive and innovative.

The practice of focusing on love, compassion, and wholeness is a continuous process of renewal and growth. It demands mindfulness and intentionality, guiding us to make choices that align with our highest values. As we persist in this endeavor, we become living examples of the change we wish to see, radiating positivity and inspiring others to follow suit.

www.ingramcontent.com/pod-product-compliance
Lightning Source LLC
Chambersburg PA
CBHW030412130626
46549CB00004B/1747